# XO Ballerina Big Sis

This book is dedicated to every young dancer out there with big dreams. If you're full of questions, doubts, or just wondering what comes next, know this: you're not alone. I've been where you are, and I'm here to help ease some of those worries and pirouette with you towards your next goal. Think of me as your Ballerina Big Sister – the one you didn't know you needed, cheering you on every step of the way.

# XO Ballerina Big Sis

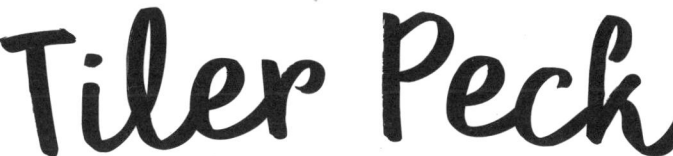

# Tiler Peck
Principal Dancer with the
New York City Ballet

with Leslie Tonner

# Contents

### Meet Your Ballerina Big Sis, Tiler Peck — 6

### Ballet School Confidential — 10
What's the first thing I should know about taking ballet? ........ 12
What is the most important quality you need as a dancer? ..... 20
Will I ever master ballet? ............................................................. 22

### In the Studio — 24
Am I paying attention? ................................................................ 26
What about posture? .................................................................. 30
My teacher doesn't like me! ....................................................... 35
Is it bad to ask questions in class? ............................................. 38
How do I handle barre-hogs and competition? ........................ 42
I can't remember the steps! ....................................................... 47
Is it okay to leave the room during class? ................................. 53

### What's Bothering Me? — 58
All I want is to be perfect! .......................................................... 60
What can I do about performance anxiety? ............................. 65
I'm obsessed with mirror-gazing. ............................................... 71
Do you compare yourself to other dancers? ............................. 76
Why does Instagram make me feel so overwhelmed? ............ 79
I'm injured! What's going to happen to me? ............................ 86

### Self-Care Strategies — 94
What can I do to feel more confident? ...................................... 96
How do you stay so positive? ..................................................... 99

| | |
|---|---|
| Help! I need to get organized! | 104 |
| Should I stretch before or after class? | 111 |
| Why is it so important to eat? | 117 |
| Am I eating enough of the right foods? | 119 |
| What can I do to get better rest and sleep? | 121 |

## Taking the Next Step — 126

| | |
|---|---|
| How do I get more stage time? | 128 |
| Should I try other styles of dance? | 132 |
| Are summer intensives worth it? | 137 |

## My Mantra, "Talent +" — 144

| | |
|---|---|
| What is "Talent +"? | 146 |

## Tiler's Hacks and Tips — 152

**Dance-bag basics** .................................................. **154**

| | |
|---|---|
| Ballet slippers | 154 |
| Pointe shoes and toe pads | 155 |
| Footcare necessities | 156 |
| Toe-shoe sewing kit and accessories | 160 |
| Massage balls | 162 |
| Therabands | 163 |
| Hair grips | 164 |
| Warm-ups | 164 |
| Snacks | 165 |
| Hydration | 166 |
| My favourite dance bag | 167 |

**Toe-shoe tutorial** .................................................... **168**

## Acknowledgements — 181

# Meet Your Ballerina Big Sis, Tiler Peck

Hi Everyone,

**I'm incredibly excited to share this book with you!**

For my whole dance career, since I was a very little girl up until right now, I have been collecting information from every person I've ever met. This includes the kids I took class with, Broadway directors, ballet superstars, fashion designers, and of course my mom and dad. And everything I learn, I put into **My Dance Bag**.

So, what *is* My Dance Bag?

It's a bag in my imagination, but it's a bag all the same. It's a place where I store all the knowledge I have learned from my years of dance. Nothing is too large or too small to be included — it's bottomless (think Mary Poppins' carpetbag!).

I always carry it with me because the day might arrive when something in there will be helpful. *So I store all the lessons and wisdom I've learned along the way — the ups and downs, the good and bad.* Someday I just may find myself in a situation

where I need to rummage around inside and come up with an answer I never thought I'd use!

Now, I may be at a point in my career where I am a Principal Dancer, have danced on Broadway, and am guest starring in an exciting new streaming series. But when it comes to learning, **I am a student forever**, and the tools I put in My Dance Bag haven't failed me yet.

This is why the book you're holding is so very special to me, because it's my gift to you – it's *your* bag, too. You have hard-won knowledge in here, and it's available to you simply by opening this book. Some of it will be exactly what you need to know; some of it may be things you already sort of know; and some of it will be, nope, I don't need to know that. Well, I'm here to tell you the day will come when you'll say, "I guess I really *did* need to know that", because it happens to me all the time.

As a student in training, I would have loved a Ballerina Big Sis to ask all of my questions. It would have meant so much to have someone to

tell me to focus on what really matters and not to worry about silly things. A Big Sis to teach me what my responsibilities should be and the best ways to carry them out. Most importantly, someone to have my back and understand me.

I see you and I'm here for you. And I'm so glad I get to share My Dance Bag with you!

XO
Your Ballerina Big Sis,

Tiler

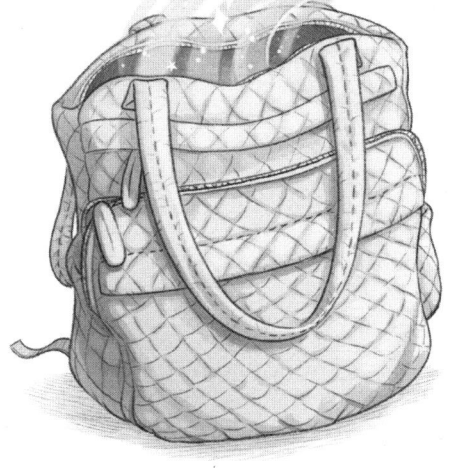

# Ballet School Confidential

# "What's the first thing I should know about taking ballet?"

*Your appearance matters. A lot. And I'm not talking about how attractive you are.*

In this book, you're going to hear me talk about **etiquette**, **good manners**, and **respect**, qualities you need in your ballet classroom as well as in life.

A big part of showing respect starts with your appearance, meaning how you look when you walk into the studio.

# YOUR APPEARANCE DEMONSTRATES RESPECT FOR YOURSELF AS WELL AS RESPECT FOR THE OTHER PEOPLE IN YOUR CLASSROOM.

If you want to get the most out of your class and *give yourself the best possible chance to succeed*, come in prepared and present yourself as someone who should be taken seriously. By that, I mean wearing form-fitting dancewear that allows the teacher and you to see your body, and pulling back your hair so it's out of your face. This shows the person at the front of the room:

# "OKAY, I MEAN BUSINESS. I'M PREPARED, AND I'M READY TO WORK."

When you're a young student, I don't think you need to come into class wearing lots of makeup.

*The most important thing about being in class is working hard and getting better.* Makeup isn't going to help with that goal and you don't want to distract from that. However, if you feel prettier or more confident when you have a little bit of makeup on, then it's okay to wear some.

*If you feel you don't need it, that's also fine – whatever helps you feel confident in your own skin.*

**When doing your hair**, you want something that is clean and up and out of your face. The most common styles are a high or low bun or a French twist. Even with something simple, there are so many ways to *make it your own*. You can do a side part, a middle part, no part, or even a fancy braid that leads into your bun. Find your own style and feel special looking like yourself instead of like everyone else in the room. You can still have stylish hair that signals:

## "I'M EAGER TO LEARN AND READY TO WORK HARD."

Obviously, if there's a uniform, then you have to wear the specified colour or style, but if not, you want to dress the way that *makes you feel like your best self*.

*Now, we all know ballet is an aesthetic art form, and the only real way to tune your instrument (your body) is to see the lines and shapes you want to make during class.*

**Whatever you wear should definitely be an extension of who you are as a person**, within reason. You don't want to hide your instrument under baggy or layered clothes.

That brings me to the topic of leg warmers: If you want to wear leg warmers, think about wearing them just at the beginning of class, while your muscles are getting warm.

# YOU, AND YOUR TEACHER, NEED TO SEE YOUR BODY'S LINES AND SHAPE TO CONTINUE WORKING ON SCULPTING AND IMPROVING.

After you finish the first few combinations at the barre, they should come off unless you are nursing an injury that needs to be kept warm. I say this because you need to be able to see your legs. *We improve by seeing ourselves make our positions and by the teacher being able to correct us.*

As for jewellery, I don't think you should wear any jewellery that is distracting. After all, you want *the focus to be on your dancing*, not on the earrings or necklace you are wearing.

In case you think this is just a matter of looking prepared, think again. Sometimes, appearance can play a key part in preparing to be an artist.

When I was about 7 years old, my teacher suggested I come to class with my fingernails painted light pink. "A manicure," she said, "changes the way you hold and use your hands. You'll be much more aware of them." So, I put pale polish on my nails – and I've never stopped doing it! She was right: The polish helped me pay **closer attention** to my fingers, which brought a delicacy and expressiveness to them. Also, a lot of times when you're stressed, the tension goes straight to your hands, and you're not always aware of that. However, when you glance at your fingers and see the pretty polish, you're reminded that the hands and fingertips are alive, and must be activated at all times. When I teach, I always emphasize that it should look like your hands and feet are speaking while you dance.

SOMETIMES, APPEARANCE CAN PLAY A KEY PART IN PREPARING TO BE AN ARTIST.

All of this is to say, *make your appearance count so you can show off what you're learning and keep track of how you are progressing.* Though I know times have changed, you can set your own personal standards for your appearance.

*You can choose to maintain a discipline that will set you on the way towards reaching your highest potential.*

# "What is the most important quality you need as a dancer?"

*Work ethic. You develop your work ethic as a dancer simply by showing up every day for class.*

There's no rank here; it applies to **everyone**. There's no class in school that teaches you this. There's nothing that can make you your best self except putting in the work. And there's always room for improvement. You will never reach a point in this profession where you can stop learning and improving. There is nothing worse than seeing a talented person who throws it away because they don't put in the work.

> THERE'S NOTHING THAT CAN MAKE YOU YOUR BEST SELF EXCEPT PUTTING IN THE WORK.

**I'm a principal dancer and go to class every day,** unless I'm injured and can't be there. The studio is where you put in the work so when you go onstage, you can just be an artist. But it's putting in the work on technique every day that's going to help you become a better version of yourself.

> YOU WILL NEVER REACH A POINT IN THIS PROFESSION WHERE YOU CAN STOP LEARNING AND IMPROVING.

Work ethic is essential and translates into every aspect of your life. Dancers tend to be diligent academic students because we have the dedication, discipline, and determination. But if you feel you're not strong in these ways, I have good news: Dance is the **perfect** place to help you work on these skills.

*A ballet career is so short, right?* So, you have to put all you have into it when you're younger. For me, it's really, really about putting in the work. It's always been that way.

# "Will I ever master ballet?"

The most important question to ask in ballet is, **"How much do you want to invest in yourself?"** Though a lot of us have talent, talent will only get you so far. To reach your fullest potential, you have to have dedication and an incredibly strong work ethic to go along with that talent. The choice is yours about how hard you want to work, but I will say that the amount of work you put in equals the amount you're going to get out of your effort.

I live by the quote, **"Always a student."** The minute you stop wanting to learn and feel you have nothing more to absorb, is the minute you're going to stunt your artistic and technical development.

Remember, class is where it starts – it's your home base. Be prepared in all the ways we're going to

discuss: Show up on time, don't walk in late, and pay attention to where you stand in the room, how you relate to others, and how you respond to your teachers. Class has been described as feeling like a sacred space where you go and put in the daily work on yourself to refine your technique and develop your artistry.

*You are the boss of how hard you're going to work in class every day; take advantage of every minute.*

To **"always be a student"** will take you far.

# In the Studio

# "Am I paying attention?"

*When a teacher is in front of the room, talking to the class, you need to pay attention because everything they say is important.*

Paying attention shows **respect**, and if you want to gain respect in the dance world, you need to also show respect to your teachers, colleagues, friends, fellow students, and yourself.

By paying attention, you will also put your best foot forward towards learning something quickly. Some people are slower learners than others, which is totally fine — we all have different learning styles. *But if you really pay attention and focus*, you're going to have a better chance of remembering the combination. Plus, a lot of teachers and directors are looking for that exact quality in a dancer! They want to see somebody who is hungry for knowledge, and **hungry to learn** more. And if you're not paying attention, you're telling them you're not really interested in learning and in what's going on.

> IF YOU WANT TO GAIN RESPECT IN THE DANCE WORLD, YOU NEED TO SHOW RESPECT TO YOUR TEACHERS, COLLEAGUES, FRIENDS, FELLOW STUDENTS, AND YOURSELF.

There's another important thing to pay attention to: **the music**. If you're fortunate enough to have live music in the classroom, you need to be very attentive to the music and the musician. Live accompaniment is a gift, and if it's there, don't take it for granted. The more attentive a listener you are, the better chance you have of being **"on the music"**. You don't want to be dancing to your own tune!

*The more you listen, the more you will train your ear and be able to pick up any tempo changes.*

Now, if you don't have live music, you should still listen very carefully to the tempo and rhythmical beat. Music gives dancers **inspiration** by telling us when to move, and sometimes, what to feel.

**Following directions** is in the same category as paying attention, and the rule here is simple:

# DON'T MAKE A TEACHER, CHOREOGRAPHER, OR DIRECTOR SAY SOMETHING MORE THAN TWICE.

You need to be in charge of holding on to that information and then implementing it. If someone constantly has to say the same thing over and over, that's not good. You're not paying attention to the person in charge of the room.

*They need to know you're listening*, because that's going to carry over and move you forward in your career.

*Everybody wants somebody who will listen.*

Now, I don't mean listening to the point of being so obedient that you become rigid and like a robot. Dancers should be able to express their own individuality; however, there is a way to listen and still attain that. To listen in a positive way shows them that you could be a **great team member** and a potentially great company member as well.

# "What about posture?"

*Posture is very important.*

*As dancers, we're used to carrying ourselves upright.* Your chest has to be forward enough so you can balance, but you have to keep your core and ribs pulled in at the same time. That's kind of tricky, keeping your ribs and core engaged and activated but still being able to breathe!

> THE WAY YOU CARRY YOURSELF IN CLASS SHOULD BE THE WAY YOU CARRY YOURSELF IN LIFE.

What I find interesting about dancers is that the minute they finish a combination, all this is over – **"We're not dancing anymore!"** – and they just collapse. The way you carry yourself in class should be the way you carry yourself in life; you don't want to walk down the street with your shoulders forward and hunched over. That kind of posture is not going to help you right now in your career, nor long term, as you continue to age.

> THE MOST IMPORTANT THING, REGARDLESS OF TECHNIQUE, IS TO ALWAYS HAVE THE ARMS ENGAGED AND HELD FROM THE BACK.

Every ballet school has their own method of training, but whether you're at a Vaganova-based school or at a conservatory that practises the Balanchine aesthetic, **the arms are always engaged and held from the back**. I tell my students that I like to imagine my shoulders are turning out just as my hips and legs do. That constant energy is felt from the back and will then translate to the arms.

Two other images my teachers passed on to me that I think you might find helpful are: "Think of jewellery and showing off a beautiful necklace you are wearing" and "When you're standing, allow yourself to feel the light (like a spotlight if you are performing) beaming on your face and body, and in return, you must feel like there is a light shining from within that needs to reach whoever is in front watching you." I am still inspired by these words today, and they have been pivotal in helping shape my stance and port de bras.

*An engaged posture is important whether you dance on your own or with a partner.*

You have to learn how to hold your arms and upper body in a way that will be beneficial to your partner. You need to let them lead and guide you, but you can't be looseygoosey, like a noodle; you must hold your carriage properly so they can do their job. **Partnering is a two-way conversation**. In order for it to be successful, both parties must hold themselves while also listening to the needs of their partner.

## *All of this begins with the way you hold your arms at the barre.*

If you've been holding your arms from the back, like we spoke of already, then you will have a head start in partnering class. That strong placement will be helpful when you need to do tricky promenades and so much more.

# "My teacher doesn't like me!"

If your teacher is constantly correcting you, coming over to fix your positions, and staring at you when the class is doing a combination, that's because they **see something in you!** They see talent, and they want to push you. Teachers notice you, pay attention to you, and spend their time trying to make you the best you can be!

TEACHERS HELP MAKE YOU
THE BEST YOU CAN BE!

This happened to me, and I will never forget it! In my first class at the School of American Ballet with Suki Schorer — a very famous, experienced teacher — she gave me five corrections before the pliés even started. I thought, "How can I already have so many when I am just standing in first position?!" She was on me and correcting me the entire class. I have to admit that I began to get really discouraged because I thought, "She doesn't like me!" After class I went home and told my mom, who is a dance teacher, what happened. She said, **"I actually think she sees your potential."**

Funnily enough, it was right after that class that Suki took me to the head of the school's office and told her she thought I needed to be moved up a level. I had no idea what was happening, but it just goes to show you that sometimes it can feel like a teacher is picking on you when they really just believe in you. They push you to make you better!

GETTING A LOT OF CORRECTIONS IS HONESTLY THE BEST WAY TO HELP YOU IMPROVE.

When you're younger, you think **close attention** and constant correcting means that your teacher sees faults in you. But there's a way to turn it around, fix it in your head, and say:

# "THANK GOODNESS THEY'RE TAKING THE TIME TO NOTICE ME AND GIVE ME CORRECTIONS."

Getting a lot of corrections is honestly the best way to help you improve. So, try not to get sad or frustrated as corrections are actually very beneficial. Now if you're not getting many corrections, try not to worry. That might just mean that the teacher doesn't see anything that needs fixing at the moment.

# "Is it bad to ask questions in class?"

*I think it is important to ask questions.*

In the ballet world, we are accustomed to **not using our voices** and we think that speaking up is a bad thing. There is always a time and a place for questions. It matters how you ask, what you ask, and when.

> THERE IS ALWAYS A TIME AND A PLACE FOR QUESTIONS.

There are some students in class (even dancers in company class!) who call out, loudly, when they don't understand something. *I do not believe that this is the most professional approach!* I believe that it's much better to **respectfully** raise your hand and wait until you're called on. You might also choose to save your questions for after class when you can be one-on-one with the teacher. You'll probably get more answers going about it that way.

**What's most important here is to understand when to use your voice.** Ask questions when you need to understand something better to help you improve as a dancer. Not just, "What count was that?" because I'm guessing the teacher already said what count it was and you just weren't listening. It's up to you, personally, to know which questions are worth asking.

**Using your voice to communicate is key.** Communication is different from just asking questions; it involves *sharing* information that helps both the person who offers it and the person who receives it. It's extremely critical that you and your teacher or your director are never left wondering, "What's going on?"

Don't be afraid to speak up if you're injured and say, "My shins are hurting a lot today and my physical therapist said I shouldn't jump for a few classes in order to give my shin splints some rest." These are the kinds of things you need to put your hand up for! *Protecting your body and your health is key.*

Letting your teacher know what is going on allows you both to be on the same page. If you don't make them aware you're hurting, they could easily think you are just being lazy and not taking the class seriously. This kind of miscommunication could lead to some very bad impressions.

# THIS IS WHY COMMUNICATION IS IMPORTANT. YOU MUST NOT BE AFRAID TO MAKE SURE EVERYONE UNDERSTANDS WHAT'S GOING ON.

# "How do I handle barre-hogs and competition?"

Barre-hogs are those people who always stand at the front barre and closest to the teacher. There is nothing wrong with wanting to put yourself in front to be seen, but everything is okay in moderation. Studio etiquette is somewhat unspoken, but the word that comes to mind is *respect*. **Respect for yourself, and respect for others.**

**IN A CLASSROOM, NORMALLY, WE DON'T HAVE SET BARRE POSITIONS OR AN ASSIGNED PLACE.**

However, if you're taking class with the same people often, there is a tendency for dancers to stand in the same barre spot every day.

*How frustrating is it if somebody takes your spot?* This is where you stand, where you feel **comfortable**. If you're the person taking a new spot, think about that for a moment. Think, why do I want to stand here, where I know that Sophia stands every single day? Don't do that to your classmate and friend.

If you've just lost your spot, you may feel frustrated. Leaving class without saying anything will make you feel unhappy and helpless. This will only hurt you in the long run. There are a couple of good ways you can handle it.

You can **speak up, nicely**, by saying something like: "You know, Heather, I really love standing at this spot. Maybe you could stand on the other side? I feel I'm able to see my progress if I stand in the same place at the barre."

**If you're not comfortable speaking to others, then talk to yourself:** "This is going to put me a little bit out of my comfort zone, but tomorrow, I'll get here a little earlier so I can get my spot back."

The alternative choice is to mope and get frustrated, but the only person you'll be hurting is yourself.

*What's vital here is to check in with yourself!*

Think about your choices and decide what you want to do. Do you want to speak up and ask for what you want? Do you want to put yourself in a different barre position that day and then fix the problem tomorrow? Or do you want to say nothing and let yourself silently struggle? Honestly, doing nothing is the worst choice of all.

Class can feel competitive and you should feel like you are putting your best foot forward. I think that where you stand can be really important. The teacher can see the entire room but will obviously have a closer look at you if you're in the front.

> THINK ABOUT YOUR CHOICES AND DECIDE WHAT YOU WANT TO DO. DO YOU WANT TO SPEAK UP AND ASK FOR WHAT YOU WANT?

**My advice is** not to stand in the back all the time, because you want to be seen as someone with the drive to learn. However, I think standing in the front of the room all the time isn't a good idea either. This might make people think that you are an attention hog who never lets anybody else take a turn.

A director or boss will *not* want someone who isn't a team player in their company community. People want to hire a **dedicated** worker who can get along with others. They want someone striving to be better. Being a collaborative part of a group is essential for a corps de ballet member. You're on a team; you have to be alert and responsive to others.

*You need to find the perfect balance. This is also a form of respect.*

Modelling respectful etiquette will help you to be your personal best while also being **mindful** of those around you. This is something we hope to be taught when we're young, but it's never too late to start learning. **You can be a determined, hard-working dancer who is also a courteous person to work with.**

YOU'RE ON A TEAM; YOU HAVE TO BE ALERT AND RESPONSIVE TO OTHERS.

# "I can't remember the steps!"

*All of us learn at a different pace.*

Some of us pick up choreography quickly, while others need extra time to let the choreography, counts, or musicality **SETTLE IN** before we return to work on them.

**Be patient with yourself.** You must not compare how long it takes you to learn the steps with how long it takes someone else. We're all different people, so remember, the pace of your learning doesn't dictate the quality of your dancing.

We are lucky to live in the digital world, with easy-to-access videos. We can watch our idols or former interpreters dance, and come away inspired by their performances. Sometimes you need to see someone else conquer a difficult role, or a series of steps, in order to gain enough confidence to try it yourself. Personally, I also use video to help me remember choreography, and to self-correct my own dancing by recording my own work in the studio.

*There have been many instances when I have watched a video of another ballerina performing a variation I dance.*

I've seen them do things I never thought were possible, and thought, "Wow, that was a beautiful choice — I want to try to incorporate that tomorrow in my variation. Maybe it will work for me, maybe it won't, but at least I know the range of possibilities since I have seen it done with my own eyes."

Now, when it comes to **remembering choreography**, watching a rehearsal that was filmed is the easiest strategy. You might think it's scary to ask your teacher for a video, but I trust they would appreciate knowing you're going to put in the extra time and effort at home.

> SOMETIMES YOU NEED TO SEE SOMEONE ELSE CONQUER SOMETHING IN ORDER TO GAIN ENOUGH CONFIDENCE TO WANT TO TRY IT YOURSELF.

## *Here's a good way to ask:*

"Would it be okay if I video the last run? I would love to keep going over the choreography and the counts *[or you can mention whatever it is you need]* while I'm at home so I can come in tomorrow and feel really secure."

I think that shows you're a **hard worker** who takes **initiative**. *There's nothing wrong with speaking up and asking for something that can really help.*

*Music is also a very helpful tool to remember steps.*

Find the music you're dancing to online. You can listen to it on your own, picture the movement in your mind, or even walk through it at home. Sometimes, when I am relearning choreography, I put on the music and my body actually remembers the steps faster than my brain can. We call this "muscle memory". If you're having a hard time remembering choreography, dig deeper into the music, and it will help lead the way.

SOMETIMES, WHEN I AM RELEARNING CHOREOGRAPHY, I PUT ON THE MUSIC AND MY BODY ACTUALLY REMEMBERS THE STEPS FASTER THAN MY BRAIN CAN.

**You can also create markers** — connect what happens in your role or variation to the specific moment in the music. For example, "I do an arabesque on this part, I chaîné on that part, and then I do grand jeté here." These markers will help the sequences seem shorter in your mind. Instead of trying to learn and remember a variation in its entirety, you can try breaking it down into sequences.

*By dividing the variation into several different parts, it will seem more attainable and manageable.*

Then, when it comes time to perform, the **preparation**, **discipline**, and **hard work** will have paid off. You won't worry as much about the technical aspects of your performances because you will know you have already put in the work in class and rehearsal. *This will allow you to move more freely and with more confidence.*

# "Is it okay to leave the room during class?"

*When to leave the room is a tricky question, because part of me wants to say, "Don't leave the room!"*

If you show up to a class, then I believe that you need to come prepared to be present for that hour and a half. If you really need to go to the toilet, or something equally necessary, then yes, of course, you should go. However, I think you only leave class if it's an emergency.

Committing to that hour-and-a-half class without interruptions is a simple way to teach yourself discipline. **Leaving the room means you're most likely going to miss out on something.** You might miss that one correction that will fix a pirouette that you haven't been able to do. You might also miss seeing a fellow classmate do something remarkable that might inspire you to try it too.

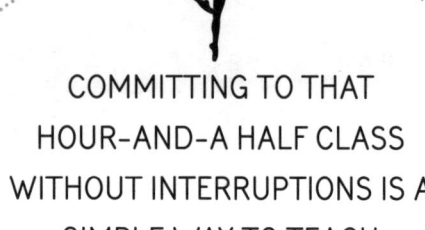

COMMITTING TO THAT HOUR-AND-A HALF CLASS WITHOUT INTERRUPTIONS IS A SIMPLE WAY TO TEACH YOURSELF DISCIPLINE.

I've been in situations where I've seen the same person leave every single day: They need water; they need the toilet. Instead of falling into that pattern, **do your best to come prepared** – bring a water bottle and try to use the toilet before class.

*There also may be times when you want a mental break. You need to ask yourself, do I want it or need it?*

If you're having a really bad moment in class that leaves you feeling defeated and like you're about to cry, perhaps stepping out of the room can be helpful. **Give yourself a little breather, and then, if you feel you're able to, walk back in with a different attitude.**

*Another way to look at this is to understand that there is power in being able to say to yourself:*

"You know, I'm feeling really defeated right now. It feels like this teacher is being extremely hard on me, and I just want to give up and cry. But I'm not going to. I'm not going to give up or give them the satisfaction of knowing that I'm upset. I'm going to take control of the situation, work on my resilience, and learn how to handle my emotions when things get challenging."

*Make it your decision:*

# "I'M GOING TO GET THROUGH THIS, AND IT WILL MAKE ME STRONGER."

Maybe you will need to walk out of the room, or maybe you'll decide not to leave and say,

## "I'M GOING TO STICK IT OUT FOR THE REST OF THIS HOUR AND A HALF, AND THEN I'LL FIND AN OUTLET TO PROCESS MY FEELINGS."

**You could try writing down your feelings** in your journal, talking to your BFF, or whatever it is you need to do to let your emotions out.

I don't know what the best answer is for you because we all react differently when we're feeling upset, *but I do know you're always better off when you know there are ways you can help yourself.*

# What's Bothering Me?

# "All I want is to be perfect!"

*I am about as much of a perfectionist as you can get!*

As ballerinas, most of us are focused on being perfectionists. We all want to hit our **technical aspects**: do the perfect triple pirouette, pull off the perfect ending to a variation. *And I think that that's what makes us great and makes us continue to try to get better.*

SOMETIMES, THE MORE IMPORTANT THING IS TO BE PRESENT IN THE MOMENT.

# AS ARTISTS, WE SHOULD WANT TO TRANSPORT THE AUDIENCE.

But I wish I could have understood when I was younger what "perfectionism" actually means. Like, **what is a perfect show?** When you do all the steps perfectly?! These questions made me start to wonder, is the only criterion for a perfect show nailing all the technical elements? *Is that really what the audience wants to see?*

Yes, I want to hit those moments, but sometimes, the more important thing is to be present in the moment, not just worried about getting from A to B to C to D. Why? Because as artists, we should want to transport the audience. *Nobody wants to see a perfect technical performance they aren't moved by.* **Dancing is much more than just perfect technique**; it's what you as an individual dancer bring to your performance.

If you find yourself thinking this way, try to notice what triggers your perfectionist mindset — is it looking at other students in the mirror, or seeing Instagram videos with dancers doing **impossible things**, or talking to your dance friends and focusing endlessly on technical tricks? You can even keep a little list of the times when you're bothered by perfectionism, and when it next happens, change your tune. *Turn off the video, change the subject with your friends,* **interrupt the cycle**. Then, give yourself a gold star in your notebook every time you don't get triggered.

# SOMETHING THAT BECOMES A BAD HABIT IS MEANT TO BE BROKEN.

*Once you figure out what bugs you, you can focus on what it is about yourself that you like.*

**Because we are our own best cheerleaders**. And remember, one dancer can turn really well, another can jump, another has a flexible back – we all, each of us, have our special skills.

*For me, the studio is where you focus on your technique, to work on being the best you can, and then you go onstage and leave it all out there.*

And sometimes there's beauty when something unexpected happens – and those are the most exciting moments, when you hold a balance you didn't mean to, or you do an extra turn – it's like surprising yourself.

As Heather Watts, a great former ballerina and a mentor of mine, always said, **"You learn the rules to then go onstage and be able to break them. For me, this means you won't worry as much about the technical aspects during a performance because you will know you have already put in the work in class and rehearsal. This way, when you get onstage, you can break free and just dance."**

This freedom allows you to channel your inner feelings and express your emotional response to the music. You can be more in touch with yourself because you're not constrained by technique.

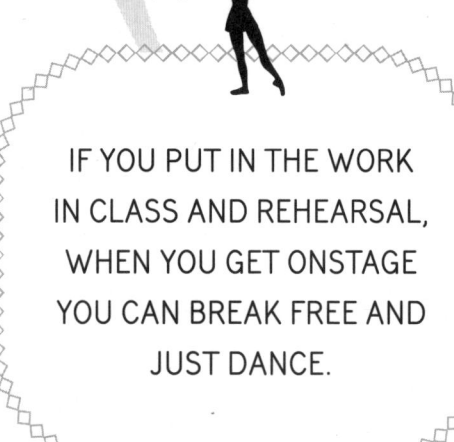

IF YOU PUT IN THE WORK IN CLASS AND REHEARSAL, WHEN YOU GET ONSTAGE YOU CAN BREAK FREE AND JUST DANCE.

# "What can I do about performance anxiety?"

*Performance anxiety can be really debilitating for some dancers* — debilitating to the point that they can't have fun onstage, or enjoy a performance because it is so nerve-racking even just being out there. *I've seen it happen, and it's not uncommon.* I feel deeply for them because a dance career is so hard that if you can't enjoy yourself once you get onstage, why would you want to put yourself through all this?

## IT'S EXTREMELY IMPORTANT TO DEAL WITH THAT KIND OF ANXIETY.

> WEEKS BEFORE MY *SLEEPING BEAUTY* SHOWS, I WOULD BE SO STRESSED THAT I FELT LIKE I DIDN'T WANT TO GO ONSTAGE BECAUSE I WAS TOO NERVOUS.

*I don't think anybody should ever be embarrassed to seek help.*

There are some amazing sports psychologists you can speak to who can help you work through those feelings. **They are here to help.** Many major professional athletes have a psychologist as part of their team to help them go out and be at their competitive best. I think that we, as dancers, can do the same; we're athletes as well.

*For me, I can speak from experience about feeling this kind of anxiety.* I am not normally a nervous performer, but *Sleeping Beauty* is a different story for me. The first few years I danced Aurora, the role made me so anxious that I used to lose sleep for a few months leading up to my performances. Weeks before my shows, I would be so stressed that I felt like I didn't want to go onstage because I was too nervous.

*And if you know me, you know that I love to perform, so this was a very unusual and difficult situation for me.*

WORKING WITH SOMEONE CAN MAKE A REAL DIFFERENCE.

The fact that some people feel that way every time they perform is something I can really sympathize with. **And again, I would strongly encourage you to get the help that you need for this;** working with someone can make a big difference.

Though we can't just make ourselves feel like, "Oh, this is so easy!", *we can find routines or words that might help*.

## *Right before I go onstage, I always tell myself, "It's just like another rehearsal."*

If you think of the show as "another rehearsal", **you won't be scared** to go for things like you do in rehearsal, when you don't have the fear of letting down the audience if you fail. You will be more **daring** and can **focus** on enjoying the moment for yourself and the person you're dancing with, rather than pleasing the people in the audience. What's beautiful about that thought is it helps take some of the pressure off that you are putting on yourself, perhaps even unknowingly.

> YOU WILL BE MORE DARING AND CAN FOCUS ON ENJOYING THE MOMENT FOR YOURSELF AND THE PERSON YOU'RE DANCING WITH.

After all, we take class and do our rehearsals without having to worry about being perfect for an audience.

Knowing an audience is watching during a performance is what makes people nervous. We feel the pressure to deliver flawlessly. I say worrying about perfection dims the joy — for both the dancer and the audience.

Yet what's so amazing about a live performance is that when you dance for yourself, you'll bring the audience along with you to a special place, one that will stay with them forever.

*But more importantly, you need to not be stressed, enjoy it yourself, and experience that feeling of floating or flying or whatever you feel when you dance.*

I want you to work on how to escape from that anxiety, with professional help, with your own words, to help de-stress, so you can feel your best and enjoy your dancing.

> WHEN YOU DANCE FOR YOURSELF, YOU'LL BRING THE AUDIENCE ALONG WITH YOU TO A SPECIAL PLACE, ONE THAT WILL STAY WITH THEM FOREVER.

# "I'm obsessed with mirror-gazing."

*There's a fine balance between using the mirror to help self-correct, as we all do during class, and being addicted to mirror-gazing, watching yourself all the time.*

One of my teachers, Sally Leland, often said, **"You can always learn something by watching others."**

You can see something you like and want to put it into your "bag" to use some way going forward, or you can notice something you don't like and want to make sure you don't make the same mistake in your own dancing. *All of this can come if you watch your fellow students or colleagues and set new goals for yourself regularly.*

As many of us are **visual learners**, myself included, I learn from watching others dance as well as watching myself. As I watch, sometimes I think, "Oh, I like the way that looked." And then, "What exactly did I like?" Or sometimes, the mirror shows me something I don't like, and then the next time I do the combination, I fix what I saw as I self-correct my work.

*By looking in the mirror, you can learn what shapes look better for you.*

For example, how much to cross a tendu (to the front or back) to give you the best line for your body, as everyone's body is different. It's important to be aware of the vantage point of the audience and what angles they will see.

**However, the mirror isn't always helpful.** Let's focus on épaulement for a moment. Something I always say to students is, "You rarely want your head to be straight forward. Most of the time, you have to have a curve of the neck." You can use the mirror to correct that yourself, but doing so will affect your eye placement, which is also crucial. Take, for instance, écarté devant. In order to be in the correct position, you need to look behind and beyond your elbow. *Épaulement is such a key part of dance, and much of it needs to be felt and not just seen in the mirror.*

> YES, YOU WANT TO LEARN FROM OTHERS, BUT OVERANALYZING YOURSELF AND OTHERS CAN LEAD TO A BIG LACK OF CONFIDENCE.

**Another problem with mirror-gazing** is that when you spend too much time and attention watching other dancers, you may start to feel **insecure** about your own dancing. Yes, you want to learn from others, but overanalyzing yourself and others can lead to a big lack of confidence.

*It is not healthy to be so self-critical that you can no longer be yourself when you dance.*

If you're using the mirror in a way that's distracting or upsetting, then I would suggest you *trust your teacher or director completely*. If this habit is becoming more of a detriment than an asset, try changing your ways and use the mirror less. After all, when you're onstage, there's no mirror in front of you, so it's important not to be too reliant on it in any event.

# YOU NEED TO KNOW WHAT IT FEELS LIKE TO DANCE, TO BE AWARE OF WHAT YOUR BODY FEELS LIKE WHEN YOU CAN'T SEE YOURSELF IN THE MIRROR.

*A mirror is a great check-in facility, but it's not something you should depend on, because it's going to get taken away.* If you learn that lesson in ballet school, it's going to be much easier later on when the mirror disappears and you are all alone onstage. You need to go beyond the mirror and learn how to focus your gaze to genuinely connect with the audience.

# "Do you compare yourself to other dancers?"

*Trust me, I'd have given up a long time ago if all I did was compare myself to some of my favourite ballerinas! But who doesn't compare themselves to others?*

You're in a studio surrounded by mirrors, and you're looking at someone in class with you, and you start thinking, oh my gosh, they have better extension, they have better feet. You automatically start to make a list of all those things you don't have!

I can't tell you how many times we've probably all gone down rabbit holes of watching ballerinas we admire and thinking, why do I even dance, I don't look anything like that?

# A HEALTHY COMPARISON WOULD BE TRYING TO HOLD A BALANCE A BIT LONGER OR JUMP A LITTLE HIGHER THAN THE DANCER WORKING NEXT TO YOU.

That's called **healthy competition** and can be used for **motivation** to work a little harder and improve your skills, right? *Seeing a classmate do something at a higher level will push you to try the same.*

> IT'S REALLY IMPORTANT FOR EVERYONE TO REMEMBER THAT THERE IS ROOM FOR MANY DIFFERENT TYPES OF BALLERINAS AND THAT WE ALL HAVE DIFFERENT GIFTS.

*When I fall into that headspace of comparing, I try to remember the strengths I do have.*

Obviously, yeah, I wish I had higher extension or that my feet could be like Sylvie Guillem's or Alessandra Ferri's. But then I start to think, if I had those things, I might not be able to turn the way I do or move at the speed at which I can.

It's really important for everyone to remember, as I said before, that there is room for many different types of ballerinas and that we all have different gifts. Each of us will get a chance to use them if we keep working hard.

# "Why does Instagram make me feel so overwhelmed?"

*What's amazing about Instagram, and the internet in general, is the amount of knowledge that is readily accessible just by looking at your phone.*

As a dancer, you can easily engage on apps with other dancers, dance professionals, or avid dance fans and see things in the dance world you might never be able to see in real life. Sometimes, it's archival videos of dancers from the past, while other times, it could be performances by companies in places very far from you, available right on your phone.

> IT'S ALSO EXTREMELY IMPORTANT TO REALIZE THAT SOCIAL MEDIA IS A SNIPPET OF SOMEBODY'S LIFE, NOT THE WHOLE PICTURE.

You can learn so much by watching other ballerinas — I know I have. But it's also extremely important to realize that social media is a snippet of somebody's life, not the whole picture. Everybody puts their best foot forward on Instagram, but a lot of it isn't entirely real. That is why I also try to share photos and videos of times when I'm down — for instance, stories showing what it's really like coming back from an injury. This way, people know that they're not alone. A ballerina's life is glamorous, but not always.

*Showing the tough times with the good is the reality of a dancer's life. It is beautiful and difficult at the same time.*

> EVERYBODY PUTS THEIR BEST FOOT FORWARD ON INSTAGRAM, BUT A LOT OF IT ISN'T ENTIRELY REAL.

Another issue is that many dancers, young and old, watch video excerpts of famous ballet "tricks" and super-challenging dance steps and think either "I'll try that!" or "I'll never ever be that good, no matter how hard I work!"

## *I have a few things to say about "tricks".*

**First of all, it's important to remember that being able to execute certain technical steps, or "tricks", does not necessarily make you a great dancer.** Yes, they are exciting and great tools to have at your disposal, but they are a portion of a dancer, not the complete package. I say this because there are some dancers who have wonderful careers who are not "tricksters", so I want to make sure you don't get disappointed and think, "'Tricks' aren't my cup of tea, so I shouldn't dance." That is not the case!

> WORK YOURSELF UP TO IT. START SLOWLY AND GRADUALLY ADD A NEW COMPONENT EACH DAY.

At the same time, if your goal is to be a virtuosic dancer, I do believe being able to perform certain difficult "tricks" would be helpful for your future.

*By "tricks", I mean something you might see on Instagram and not something you are taught in class.*

These are things you need to work up to and only do in a studio, not in your room at home.

*A new "trick", like a difficult lift or a challenging turn or jump, is going to take a lot of trial and error.*

The best way I can put it is, work yourself up to it. Meaning start slowly, and gradually add a new component each day. The best option would obviously be to ask a friend or classmate who already knows how to execute the "trick" to demonstrate and help teach you. However, I know that this isn't always possible and that many dancers attempt things on their own. **If you're going to try something new alone, please try to make sure that whatever "trick" you are trying to do is in reach of your level**, because if not, this is the quickest path to getting injured.

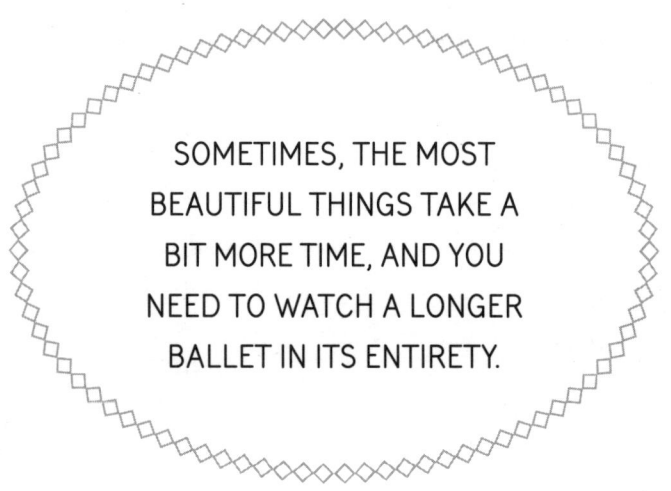

> SOMETIMES, THE MOST BEAUTIFUL THINGS TAKE A BIT MORE TIME, AND YOU NEED TO WATCH A LONGER BALLET IN ITS ENTIRETY.

There's another important lesson about all those videos of famous ballet "tricks". **Our attention spans are so much shorter now**, and we just want to swipe through and see a short video or something exciting, like the Black Swan 32 fouetté turns. However, I would venture to say if that's the case, then you most likely missed what *you can really learn by watching*. Sometimes, the most beautiful things take a bit more time, and you need to watch a longer ballet in its entirety.

*This allows you to see the artistry unfold and learn what makes a performance great from beginning to end, or even understand why classical ballet is relevant.*

*Just like it takes time to grow as an artist, you need to take time choosing and absorbing what you see in dance.* This way, you can make your social media time a true learning experience. Then, if you want a break, you can watch a video of whatever makes you smile or touches your heart.

My message to you is, do not let social media overrun your life. It should **only enhance it**, and when you get to a point of feeling overwhelmed, take a beat and try to remember it's not reality. I always say that everything is okay in moderation, and it is the same rule for the amount of time you should allow yourself to be on social media. Instagram can be a wonderful asset in learning about dance and being able to explore so much, but in the end, bring yourself down to reality and remember that Instagram is not the be-all and end-all.

DO NOT LET SOCIAL MEDIA OVERRUN YOUR LIFE.

# "I'm injured! What's going to happen to me?"

*You're going to have injuries, and when you do, you will feel like you've hit rock bottom.*

*I've been really lucky I haven't suffered many injuries*, but the ones I have had have been quite serious. A few years ago, I found out that I had a herniated disc in my neck that left me unable to fully move my head for 6 months. **At that moment, I felt the world was over.**

**I saw half a dozen different doctors** who all told me I needed surgery or would never dance again. They said that without surgery, I ran the risk of potential paralysis if I were to get knocked into a certain way because my disc was protruding so much, it was touching my spinal cord.

> I DID NOT STOP SEARCHING FOR ANOTHER PHYSICIAN BECAUSE I DIDN'T BELIEVE I HAD FOUND A DOCTOR WHO WAS REALLY LISTENING TO ME.

I did not stop searching for another physician because I didn't believe I had found a doctor who was really listening to me and treating me as the patient rather than just treating my MRI image.

With that search came a seventh doctor, and that was Dr Frank P. Cammisa, Jr, at New York's Hospital for Special Surgery, where they specialize in orthopaedics.

*He was the first doctor who I felt really heard me.*

After physically evaluating me, he sat with my physical therapist, Marika Molnar, and me in his office for about 45 minutes and talked through options. He told me he didn't like to rush into surgery with his professional athletes, and if I had the time, he would suggest waiting to see if anything would improve on its own. He didn't say for certain that it would, but he did say that discs can heal and reabsorb on their own, if given time. So, while he didn't tell me it definitely would heal, he did say, "Let's wait and see if the body **heals** before rushing to any drastic conclusions."

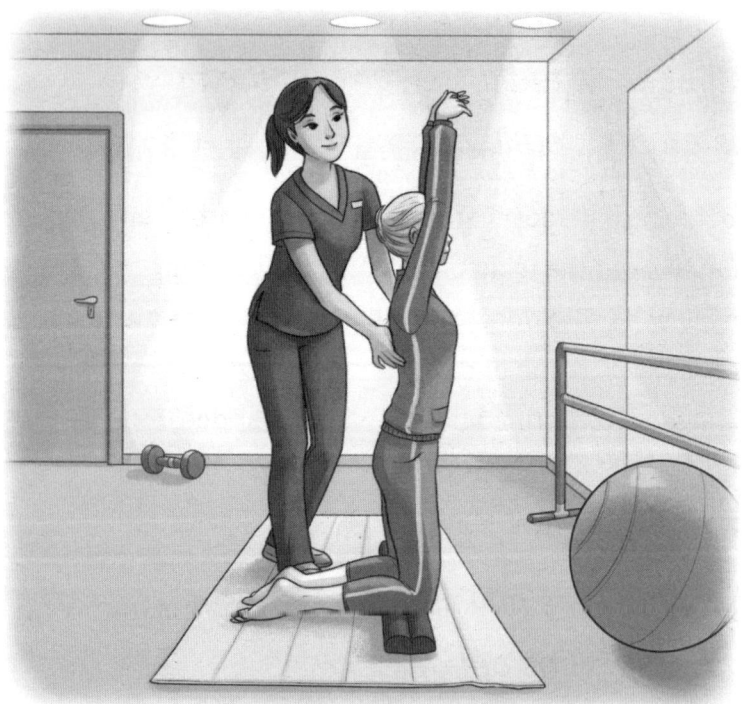

> "LET'S WAIT AND SEE IF THE BODY HEALS BEFORE RUSHING TO ANY DRASTIC CONCLUSIONS."

*At that moment, I felt so grateful that a doctor actually was taking the time to listen and really see <u>me</u>.*

Fast forward, I gave it time, and it reabsorbed enough for him to clear me to go back to physical therapy and work my way back to dancing. I will be forever grateful to him for really listening and giving me facts and possibilities. I came to him terrified because the other doctors had made me fearful for my future, and he calmly and professionally guided me to the best choices.

*I can't stress how important it is not to make any decisions out of fear.*

> I WILL BE FOREVER
> GRATEFUL TO HIM FOR
> REALLY LISTENING AND
> GIVING ME FACTS
> AND POSSIBILITIES.

During the time I was in recovery, I had a number of **different therapies,** including **physical therapy** and **energy healing**. Both helped me focus on growing stronger physically and mentally. One of the hardest things was training myself to sleep on my back, with pillows placed under my arms. This posture is what my physical therapist advised was the best way to heal the neck, because it takes the strain off the neck and the nerves that run down your arms. This was the only sleeping position where I didn't feel the nerve pain I was experiencing down my arms.

> WHEN YOU'RE AT YOUR LOWEST POINT, THAT CAN BE THE MOST IMPORTANT AND VITAL TIME OF CHANGE. THAT'S WHEN THE ARTISTIC GROWTH COMES.

*Even today, I still use heating pads, do certain exercises, and sleep with a specific pillow* to continue to protect my body from any stress on my neck. Remember, my perfect pillow isn't necessarily your perfect pillow. Yet I was able to come back, very slowly, and, ultimately, dance.

It is vital to your recovery that exercises prescribed by your physical therapist be done. **You have to hold yourself accountable** and put that into practice. Thinking that an injury will heal just by going to physical therapy isn't always the case. If you're not actually doing the exercises that they prescribe for you to do on your own time, then you will only be hurting yourself. If you want to heal quickly and fully, then you have to put in the work to heal as well.

*Injuries are the moments you feel are going to break you.*

**When you're injured, you think the world's ending.** But when you're at your lowest point, that can be the most important and vital time of change. That's when the artistic growth comes.

*So, when you get into those moments of despair over having an injury, I want you to remember:*

 It's easy to say, "Find the beauty in it", but it's totally miserable to be there. This is true for everyone.

 When you're at the bottom, another side will emerge – it will come! – bringing its own surprising rewards.

 You will learn so much about yourself, and it will stay with you as you learn and grow.

Believe me, what you learn and gain during your recovery will come through in your dancing. There's no way that your growth as a person will not affect the way you dance and how you come across to your audience. The amount of artistic growth and depth I found in my dancing after injuries was because I found more growth within myself. And that shines through when you're dancing.

# Self-Care Strategies

# "What can I do to feel more confident?"

*Another part of in-class learning is working on building your confidence.*

First, you can work on your confidence by not being afraid to make mistakes and even to fail. *You never know what you're capable of until you try,* and there's no one who hasn't experienced some kind of failure in ballet! It's a very challenging and difficult art form.

**However, learning from mistakes is where you will find your greatest growth as a dancer.** In the classroom, try putting yourself forward in a combination you've never done or one you are having trouble with — it's really okay if it doesn't go well. Every time you try something, you will be

1. Little me at 3, flexible even then, and always smiling.

2. Three years old, and here comes trouble! You can see that I was a performer right from the start.

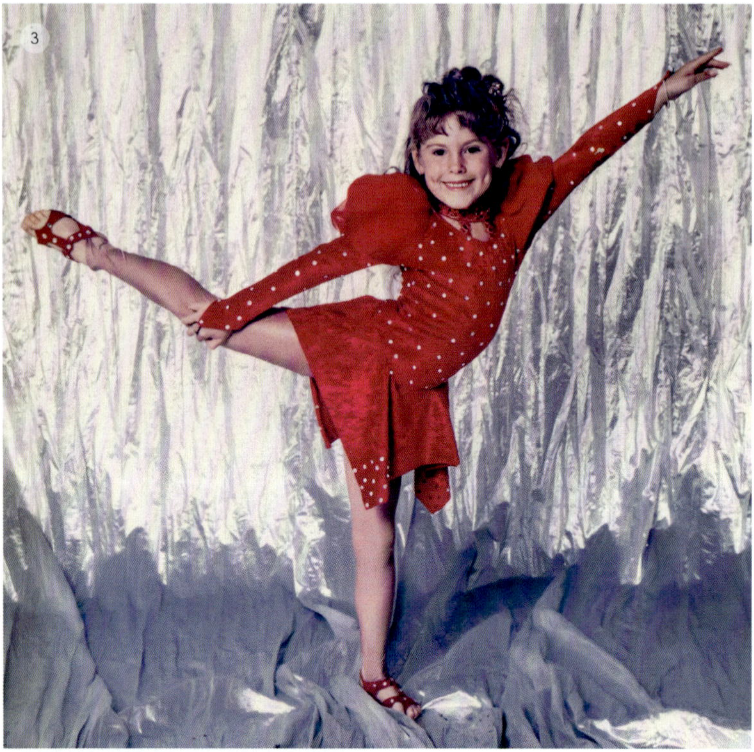

Photo by Tiler's mom

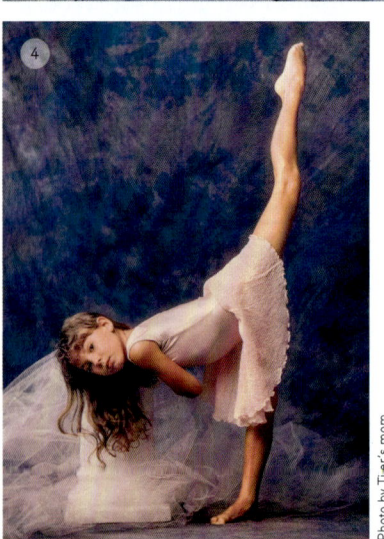

3. This is from one of my first lyrical solos, performed at age 5, which my mom actually choreographed for me. How special it was that my mother was my first dance teacher, and the person who gave me my foundation in dance.

4. Apparently I took dance very seriously, even at age 7!

5. Clearly I was not only ready for my close-up at age 8, I was there to help my friends look their stage-worthy best. I still am!

6. I'm 9 and dancing Clara in the *Radio City Rockettes Christmas Spectacular* in California.

7. Told you I was a toughie! I'm 10 and shooting a *Power Rangers* TV commercial.

8. My beloved teacher, Suki Schorer, helped make me the dancer I am today in so many important ways. This is when I was 11 and first began to attend the School of American Ballet, while I had a role on Broadway in *The Music Man*.

9. One of the few photos of 12-year-old me sitting still, looking very serious, and making sure my legs and feet looked just right.

Photo by Erin Baiano

10. Baby ballerinas! Yes, that's ABT star Isabella Boylston – Bella to her friends – and me sharing a dressing room backstage at a gala after recently becoming young principal dancers. We call ourselves "ballerina besties from across the plaza". That's right, you can be in rival companies and be great friends!

11. Perhaps my #1 full-length ballerina role is the mischievous Swanilda, who leads the audience through a humorous love triangle using acting, mime, and, of course, dance to tell the story.

12. Here I'm performing a beautiful pas de deux from Jerome Robbins's *Other Dances*. I love the freedom I feel when dancing this ballet.

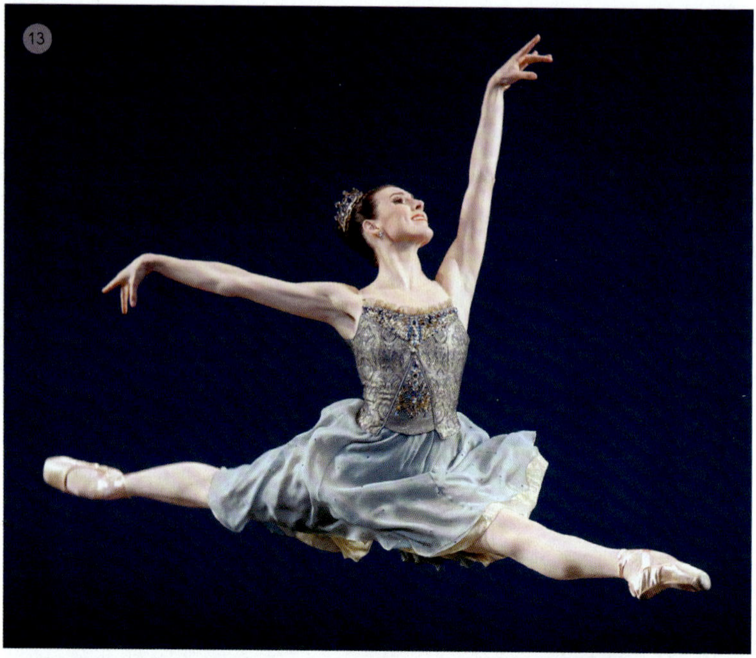


Photo by Erin Baiano

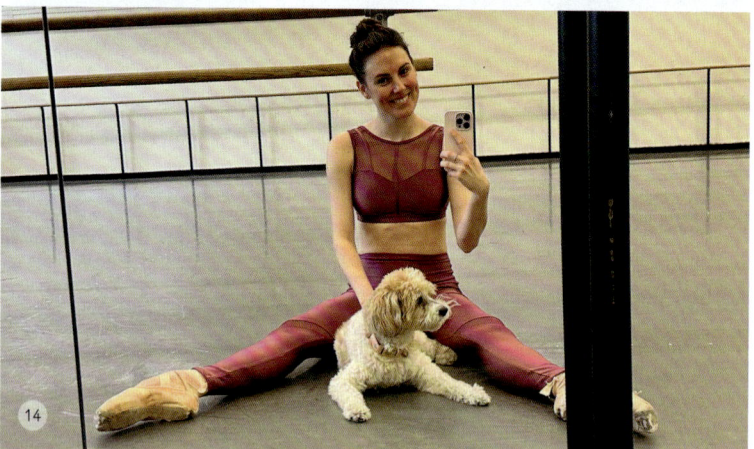

13. Flying high in another great Balanchine ballet, *Tschaikovsky's Piano Concerto No. 2*. It is absolutely exhilarating to dance!

14. This is me and my Cali girl. She was a real lady and my best ballerina companion ever. We travelled the world and spent many hours in the dance studio together. Wherever I went, she went!

able to apply what you learned the next time you try the step. When you see yourself conquer that troublesome step, your confidence will soar!

YOU CAN WORK ON YOUR CONFIDENCE BY NOT BEING AFRAID TO MAKE MISTAKES AND EVEN TO FAIL.

*Here's another tip to boost confidence.*

When a teacher gives a combination in centre that you've just quickly learned in class, challenge yourself to go in the first group. This is a very good way to test yourself, because if you go first, you have to know that combination. You don't want to always stand in the back and watch the first group so you have

another chance to go over it. **Pushing yourself to go first is an easy way to see how you're doing**, a kind of self-study test, as well as a challenge. Not to mention, once you see you remembered it, you will automatically feel your confidence and trust in yourself grow.

**The biggest improvement comes when we put ourselves forward to try something more.** This applies not only to classes but to performing, taking on roles, and the times when you need to get up in front and show what you've learned. With this newfound faith in yourself, never be an understudy in the back and think that you will not go on. You have to think, I need to learn this so that when my name is called, I can step in because I know that ballet. There are so many stories where an understudy goes in and does even better than the person they replaced, and then they become the star.

At the very least, you will be noticed!

*Playing it safe will only get you so far*, so I challenge you to take risks and be daring. **Always try for more and see how far that will take you!** We always want to have something more to aim for, and setting your sights higher, even in small ways, will help you feel you can rise to a challenge. **You can do it!**

# "How do you stay so positive?"

*In an art form like ballet, it's easy to go down a dangerous path of negativity.*

Dance is a discipline that judges you on how you move and how you look, which is maximized especially by the fact you are working in a room surrounded by mirrors. If you allow yourself, *it's easy to get caught in a downward spiral of comparing yourself to others and constantly finding fault with yourself.*

> IT'S CRUCIAL TO REMEMBER THAT "THE PERFECT PERSON" DOESN'T EXIST.

Sometimes, in class, you can get discouraged about a step you can't do, or a teacher you think doesn't like you as much as another student, or a feeling that your body isn't exactly the way you want it to be.

*Whatever it is, I am here to say these are all natural things that go through our heads.*

**None of us are perfect human beings with every part of ourselves exactly right.** It's crucial to remember that "the perfect person" doesn't exist, and every single person has faults and challenges of their own. That's human nature!

*I believe the easiest way to stay positive is to stay focused – yes, they're connected!* You can start by setting goals for yourself, then working to reach them. Push the negative thoughts aside and stay on the path towards reaching your goal.

Your goal can be larger, like a role in a school performance, or a scholarship to a summer programme, or an audition for a competition. Or it can be smaller, but **equally important**, like mastering a step sequence that's challenging you, learning a new jump, or figuring out a complicated musical phrase that you have trouble counting.

> WE ALL MUST CONTINUE TO GROW AND EVOLVE, AND LIVING LIFE AND OVERCOMING OBSTACLES WILL JUST ENRICH YOU.

In my deepest, darkest moments, like when I was injured and didn't know if I would be able to dance again, I found a way to turn the situation around in my head. *I made the decision to use all of the knowledge I was learning about my body through the injury, like how vulnerable I was, and bring it into my dancing.* Even when I felt like I had to relearn everything all over again, I was determined to emerge a better and different dancer on the other side of this injury. After all, who wants to remain the same dancer their entire career? We all must continue to grow and evolve, and living life and overcoming obstacles will just enrich you.

*Turning a negative into a positive might be easier for some people than others.*

If you're the kind of person who tends to be anxious and feel easily upset, it may be a bit harder to make that shift. However, if you can **learn to keep your eye on the bigger goal** – how you are going to reach your personal success and what you can do to make a difference – you can really find your balance when challenging or defeating thoughts creep in.

*Because you can make a difference!*

You have the power to change your own perspective and not waste time on negativity. Put all of your time and energy into staying on track to reach your goals.

# STAY POSITIVE, STOP TRYING TO PLEASE OTHERS OR LOOK LIKE OTHERS, AND THINK ABOUT YOURSELF. YOU'RE WORTH IT!

# "Help! I need to get organized!"

*For me, and for many dancers who are disciplined students, our organization and work ethic carry over into every aspect of our lives.*

I'm certain this will carry over into your studies in school. A lot of teachers have said some of their best pupils were ballet students, because we have the **discipline** and **determination** to work ingrained in us.

However, I also know dancers who have a hard time multitasking; they struggle with *compartmentalizing* and can only really focus on one thing at a time. Some dancers have a hard time finishing school while they're intensively studying dance, but it's important to know you can, and it is doable!!!

*My best advice is to give yourself a schedule.*

> IF YOU DON'T SCHEDULE YOUR TIME WELL, YOU MIGHT START PROCRASTINATING, WHICH WILL LEAD TO FEELING (OR BEING) OVERWHELMED.

If you're enrolled in school and you're studying dance, you already have a lot going on. By creating a schedule, **you're then allowing yourself to have time off to relax and just breathe**. That is so important! I call it Down-Time Organization. A lot of people need time allocated to just relax, for both their bodies and their minds. *Even doing nothing for a while can help!* Otherwise, you find yourself taking class, going to school, doing homework, and feeling like you never get a break. If you don't schedule your time well, you might start procrastinating, which will lead to feeling (or being) overwhelmed. You then have a higher risk of feeling burned out or spread too thin: **"How am I going to make all of this work?"**

I was always the type of person who loved school and actually had to do my homework on my 3-hour car ride to and from dance class every day. *However, I was always good at multitasking and realize that might be easier said than done for others.* As my career started blossoming and my workload became more challenging, that's when I began to look at my schedule the way I looked at my work in ballet.

YOU THINK, "HOW AM I GOING TO REMEMBER THIS LONG AND DIFFICULT 20-MINUTE PIECE AND FIND THE STAMINA?"

**Here's how I did it:** Any ballet can feel daunting, even overwhelming, and you think, "How am I going to remember this long and difficult 20-minute piece and find the stamina?" *I started to break the ballets down.* George Balanchine's *Tarantella*, for example, is an 8-minute virtuosic ballet that is extremely hard to get through because it is jam-packed technically, and quite exhausting. **You have to move at a very fast pace while doing difficult choreography.** Instead of looking at this ballet as 8 minutes of exhaustion, I took it apart.

To handle *Tarantella*, I look at it as four entrances for the ballerina. By breaking the ballet down in terms of the entrances, *some of the overwhelming pressure begins to be taken off*. As soon as I exit after my first solo, I stand in the wings and tell myself, "Only three more to go."

*When you approach a ballet this way, you're learning to count down rather than looking at this uphill battle that seems never-ending.*

By **"organizing"** my time within the ballet, it doesn't feel so hard to dance. That's how I began to see that time management worked the same way.

Ask yourself, "How can I divide my time so I can get the most done while still allowing myself to have some fun?" Break your day into sections as needed and be sure to work in some breaks. **Have a schedule in mind for whatever you do.**

After you attend your school classes, get to class early enough to warm up and do your pre-class exercises, and leave time after class to stretch while your muscles are still warm and you can wind down. By maximizing your studio time, like including stretching, for example, then you already have that done for the day, which allows room for other things.

*Remember to give yourself some time between activities.*

> **IF YOUR GOAL IS TO DANCE PROFESSIONALLY, TIME ORGANIZATION WILL BE ONE OF THE MOST HELPFUL THINGS YOU CAN DO FOR YOURSELF.**

If your goal is to dance professionally, time organization will be one of the most helpful things you can do for yourself. Your work time will be heavily scheduled, and you'll need to be super-organized with whatever time you have left. And if you are planning to go to university, you'll find organization an extremely valuable skill.

# "Should I stretch before or after class?"

*When you're younger, you think, "Oh, it's fine, my body can just do it all."*

The truth is, you must **be kind to your body** when you're young because that carries over and gives you the longevity in your career that we all want.

Dancers are all different, and each dancer needs something different for their body. You should work to find what exercises will help your body, not someone else's.

*As for when to warm up and stretch, everyone is a little different.*

*I like to get to class half an hour early to do my routine.* I start with simple exercises that I do lying down on my back and with my feet on the wall. My physical therapist loves this because I am able to watch and see what happens to my feet as I am doing the exercises. I start by **lifting my toes**, and, yes, that means all 10, which includes the pinky toes, even though they are the hardest to lift! I raise and release them about 10 times. Then, I **flex my ankles** (keeping the toes relaxed and not flexed) to get the ankles moving and the talus (your large ankle bone) gliding properly.

*Again, I do this about 10 times.*

ALL OF THESE THINGS HELP MY FEET GET WARM BEFORE HAVING TO JUMP INTO PLIÉS AT THE START OF CLASS.

Next, I add the toes so the ankles and toes are all flexed, and I do a **little flex and release** about 10 times. Finally, I do a little **demi-pointe prance action** (lifting the heels up) one foot at a time, so that all of the tendons begin to move, glide, and stretch. I also use a **heating pad** on my calf to warm it, and then I roll it out with a small bouncy ball. All of these things help my feet get warm before having to jump into pliés at the start of class. *I like to think of it as my very own "mini-class" before actual class.*

## *Some people do core strengthening before class, like planks; some people stretch.*

Dancers who are really flexible stretch a lot, I find. It seems that dancers like to do what they are good at, but I **challenge you to do the opposite**. If you're naturally flexible, chances are you need to stretch less and strengthen more, and vice versa. Personally, I have a lot of strength and less flexibility, so most of my time needs to be spent on stretching and lengthening. With that said, I prefer to stretch after class, because I think it's better to stretch while my muscles are warm, reducing the possibility of pulling a muscle. Remember, that's coming from a dancer who is a little bit tighter!

Dancers are all different, and each dancer needs something different for their body. You should work to find what exercises will help your body, not someone else's.

For me, **Gyrotonics** and **Pilates** are great supplementary types of exercises that I think complement ballet, as the goal is to produce the same long and lean muscles that dancers want.

If possible, I do think that some private sessions are the best way to do either, so you can have someone work "hands on" with you.

**It's always best to start learning this kind of exercise with a professional trainer, not on your own.**

*When deciding what is best to focus on, start by assessing your strengths and weaknesses.*

Remember, even though we want to showcase our strengths, **working on our weaknesses is what helps us improve**. As dancers and athletes, it's important for us to understand that our bodies are all built differently, so there is no one-size-fits-all perfect guidebook to follow.

Try to find a physical therapist, trainer, or teacher who can give you specific advice on what kind of stretching, exercises, or cross-training work they believe your body would benefit from the most. We are all different in movement, style, and appearance, and how our bodies function is unique to each one of us!

> OUR BODIES ARE ALL BUILT DIFFERENTLY, SO THERE IS NO ONE-SIZE-FITS-ALL PERFECT GUIDEBOOK TO FOLLOW.

# "Why is it so important to eat?"

*In this incredible art form where we stare at ourselves in the mirror every single day, we obviously all think everybody else's body is more perfect than ours. Right?*

Of course, *there are different body types*, but the beauty is that there's room for many different ballerinas. I do think there is an essential aesthetic we should continue to strive for, and **good nutrition** can help. Plus, it's really important to talk about how nutrition goes hand-in-hand with helping to *prevent injuries* as well as helping the body to heal.

> YOU ARE NEVER GOING TO HAVE THE STRENGTH TO GET THROUGH THIS TYPE OF CAREER WITHOUT TAKING CARE OF YOUR BODY AND NOURISHING IT.

*You cannot sustain such a physically demanding career without making sure that you're well-nourished.*

However, we do live in a time when eating disorders can be triggered in young dancers because they want their body to look a certain way.

Please always keep in mind that you are never going to have the strength to get through this type of career without taking care of your body and nourishing it the way it needs to be to keep you going. **This is something that is so very important and must be ingrained in everyone from a very young age.**

# Am I eating enough of the right foods?

I try to combine fruits and vegetables with protein for each meal, and that might include **breakfasts** of oatmeal and fresh fruit, scrambled eggs and fruit, or even yoghurt parfaits with a healthy cereal for crunch and lots of different fruits. **Lunch has to be simple**; I prefer sandwiches, usually peanut butter on whole-wheat bread (or sunflower butter if you have a peanut allergy), or any good protein – turkey, tuna, egg salad – with avocado for healthy fats and iron. **For dinner**, I am partial to pasta, especially the nights before performances, when I carb load. It gives me extra energy to burn! You can add chicken to up the protein levels.

I supplement my diet between meals with Greek yoghurt, a special favourite of mine for its high protein, apples, bananas, nuts, and energy bars. My favourite are Clif Bars, and they make a version especially for kids. Another good option is RX bars. *Protein is super important* because of the high demand dancing puts on your muscles. Yoghurt also contains magnesium, as do pumpkin seeds, almonds, spinach and leafy greens, and avocados.

*Magnesium helps with muscle function, energy metabolism, and strong bones.*

# "What can I do to get better rest and sleep?"

*Dance training and performing is physically and mentally exhausting.*

I'm here to tell you that it's the same for students and professional dancers: We never seem to get as much rest and sleep as we feel we need. Luckily, here are some ways to improve the amount you get that have been helpful to me.

> TRY TO REST YOUR BRAIN AS WELL AS YOUR BODY.

> WHEN YOUR BODY IS
> AT REST, THAT IS WHEN
> THE MOST HEALING
> HAPPENS.

**First**, when you take breaks during the day, whether it's in school, during class, or in the evening, try to rest your brain as well as your body. **Try not to automatically reach for your phone, which I know we all tend to do.** Lie down on your back and practise deep breathing. Take a slow breath in through your nose, letting the air go down into your lungs, then exhale evenly out through your nose again, keeping your mouth shut.

*Several rounds of mindful breathing can rest your body and brain in a really good way.*

My physical therapist always says that when your body is at rest, that is when the most healing happens.

THE WORST THING TO DO RIGHT BEFORE BED IS TO LOOK AT ANY SCREENS, LIKE YOUR TV OR PHONE.

**Second**, try to find a good routine before bed and try not to eat right before you go to sleep. Don't eat sugary foods at night, especially not within an hour of bedtime. No caffeine, and this means caffeinated tea, coffee, and a number of sodas. Don't do anything overstimulating, like playing video games or watching TV. And try not to watch TV in the room you sleep in, so your body knows that the bedroom is a room of rest. The worst thing to do before bed is to look at any screens, like your TV or phone.
*I know this sounds like it might be a difficult change, but I challenge you to try and see what results you get.*

**Third**, after you have done a relaxing activity like reading, before you go to sleep – I'd say 15 or 20 minutes before – close your eyes and do another round of breathing. You can listen to soft music (nothing you perform or do class to!) and try to let the breathing become what occupies your thinking. Some people even put on a little meditation app that can talk you through slow, deep breathing if you find that helpful. Keep the room dark and on the cool side for better sleep.

> LISTEN TO YOUR BODY AND SEE WHAT YOU NEED FOR YOURSELF.

## *Many of us need different amounts of sleep.*

I know it is recommended that we get at least 7-8 hours of sleep, but I personally don't feel rested unless I get 9 hours. So, listen to your body and see what you need for yourself. I know that's not always possible in our overcrowded lives, handling academic school, ballet school, homework, and everything else you need to do.

*Rest and sleep are very important for your health, and the right habits can get you into a good routine that will last the rest of your life.*

# Taking the Next Step

# "How do I get more stage time?"

*You must try your hardest to make sure you have stage time before you even think about entering a company.*

Having that **experience** can be a major part of what helps you get ahead. I know it's difficult because some schools don't have many performance opportunities: they have one end-of-year showcase, and that's it. *So, I understand how tough it is for you.*

> GETTING STAGE TIME ALLOWS YOU TO BUILD YOUR CONFIDENCE, WHICH I THINK IS PIVOTAL IN ORDER TO ENTER A COMPANY.

*The question becomes, should you go the competition route or not?*

That's a pretty big decision and needs to be addressed by your family, your dance teachers, and your ballet school. Whatever choice you end up making, keep in mind that getting stage time allows you to build your confidence, which I think is pivotal in order to enter a company.

> YOU WANT TO FEEL THAT THOSE NERVES ARE GONE BECAUSE YOU'VE BEEN THERE AND DONE IT ALREADY.

*You don't want your first time onstage to take place when you are already in the company.*

You want to feel that those nerves are gone because you've been there and done it already. It's really good to have to put yourself out there in front of strangers, not just classmates, teachers, or people you know.

Performing as a student is a really great strength-building exercise. It gives you the confidence you need to be your best self and artist onstage. These experiences allow you to build your **self-esteem** gradually.

> TRY TO WORK
> YOURSELF UP TO
> THE IDEA OF GOING
> ONSTAGE LITTLE
> BY LITTLE.

If it's your first time performing within a company and you haven't had much stage time, it can feel like going from 0 to 100 in an instant. Remind yourself that nerves are normal and try to channel your nervous energy into excitement.

# "Should I try other styles of dance?"

*It's very important to try a variety of dance styles, even if all you want to do is classical ballet when you grow up.*

Having **diverse training** will help you decide what type of dancer you ultimately want to become: a ballet dancer, a Broadway dancer, or perhaps even a commercial dancer. There are so many wonderful career opportunities and, regardless of the style you decide, well-rounded training will strengthen your abilities. All dance styles positively influence one another and will help you become a more confident performer.

# VERSATILITY IS IMPORTANT, AND KNOWING OTHER STYLES WILL HELP YOU DANCE WITH MORE FREEDOM.

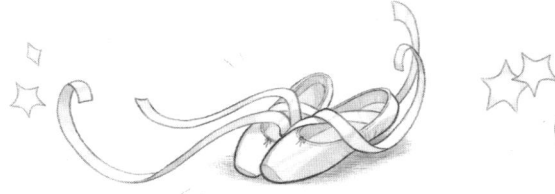

*We all know that ballet class teaches wonderful technique, but you can't possibly learn everything you need to know about dance in any one class.*

A ballet class is the best place to work on your technique and proper placement no matter what kind of dancer you are. On the other hand, a jazz or contemporary class is where you learn to dance off your axis and move a little more freely. Yes, proper technique is important. But I think it's extremely important not to be fixated on only one style as both will be beneficial in your dance career.

*If you want to dance in a classical company today, it is imperative to be a well-rounded dancer.*

More and more choreographers are creating contemporary works even for the most classical of companies. A versatile background allows the dancers to be more adaptable and able to pick up choreography more quickly.

PUT YOURSELF OUT THERE BECAUSE YOU'RE ONLY GOING TO GROW FROM THAT EXPERIENCE, EVERY SINGLE TIME.

So, throw yourself into something new even if it might scare you. You're only going to grow from putting yourself out there and learning from that experience, every single time. Am I saying that a well-rounded background might help you land a place in a ballet conservatory, a trainee programme, a second company, or even a professional job?

## YOU'LL NEVER KNOW UNTIL YOU TRY!

# "Are summer intensives worth it?"

*Summer programmes are very important.*

**Their value is more than just the obvious one – that they help advance your technical ability and performing experience.** Summer programmes are a great way to be seen by the schools that you're interested in for full-time training. For those weeks you attend, you're testing the water, getting a look at your peers from all around the country, and maybe even getting a foot in the door for your future. *All of this can play an important role moving forward in your career.*

During a summer intensive you'll be at a given place for a certain number of weeks before having to commit to a full year-long term or contract. This is an excellent opportunity to see what company style best suits you, as many intensives are attached to major companies. The Royal Ballet, English National Ballet, Northern Ballet, and Birmingham Royal Ballet are just a few companies that have schools affiliated with them, but there are so many more to choose from. With that said, if you're able to go to three different programmes over three summers then it will be much easier for you to know which one you want to attend for a year-long term.

*This way, you can commit without having to worry about whether you'll fit in and thrive in the new environment.*

BEING SURROUNDED BY TALENT IN A FRESH ENVIRONMENT IS THE BEST WAY TO IMPROVE.

**Another reason summer intensives are important** is because you get to experience working alongside students who aren't normally your familiar year-term students. Being surrounded by fresh talent in a new environment is the best way to improve, because you're pushed forward by your peers and, in the case of a company, your colleagues. A summer intensive allows you to be with **new people** and to be trained by **different teachers**, which is helpful because you don't want to get too comfortable with what you already know. If you're going to the same school year after year, you become familiar with what those teachers like and what their combinations are going to be. *By putting yourself into unfamiliar circumstances and surroundings, you're pushing yourself to take the next steps to advance your training – to learn how to excel in a new environment.* Think of it as another useful form of flexibility that involves the courage to handle change.

> SOME STUDENTS DO NEED A LONGER TIME AT HOME IN ORDER TO THRIVE, YET OTHERS DO JUST FINE GOING AWAY AT A YOUNGER AGE.

## *At what age should you start attending intensives?*

**I would say the first step in answering this question is asking your teachers if they think you are ready.** I have unfortunately seen some teachers say no just because they want to hold on to the talented dancer for themselves; however, I am hopeful that your teachers will want to see you flourish and give you their honest opinion. After you talk to your teachers and see if they think you're ready, it's okay to start thinking about going to look around.

Some students do need a longer time at home in order to thrive, yet others do just fine going away at a younger age. *This has to be a decision that the whole family makes* because it involves not only talent but also how mature you are as an individual. If you can handle the stress and homesickness that might come along with leaving home, and your family can manage it financially, then I think it's a wonderful opportunity.

*Personally, I started going to summer intensives when I was 12, which might be too soon for some students.*

**Remember, it really depends on you.** Every student is different, so it is hard to pick a certain age. I wouldn't want to stunt the growth of a talented dancer and hold them back just because of age. At the same time, I wouldn't want a dancer to be pushed to go to a summer intensive before that student is ready to be away from their familiar surroundings. There are programmes that provide housing, but going alone is a big step forward in independence if you're on the younger end. So, perhaps you might want to see if there are other students you know who might be attending. Sometimes relatives can take turns living with a small group in a new place, just for those summer weeks. For my first summers at the School of American Ballet, I lived with my grandma, and then for my third one, I decided I felt ready to stay in the dorms. There are so many ways to tailor your experience to make a summer intensive feel right for you, but I suggest you make the decision a whole family affair.

**SUMMER INTENSIVES CAN BE EXTREMELY VALUABLE IN TAKING THE NEXT STEP TOWARDS A CAREER IN DANCE.**

# My Mantra, "Talent+"

# "What is 'Talent+'?"

*As we come to a close, I hope you have learned some insightful and helpful tools that you can incorporate into your life.*

Sometimes, I feel we are just expected to know all of this information and how to navigate it, and that shouldn't be the case. *After all, who doesn't need a little help from a friend or a big sister!?* I know I do!

**My goal is to share all of my knowledge to help you succeed to the best of your ability.** I want you to remember that these are all useful tools that work for me, which doesn't mean that they *all* have to work for you. As I said in the beginning, my intention is to help you create your own custom Mary Poppins bag that you can reach into whenever you like.

> THE MOST IMPORTANT TAKEAWAY I HOPE YOU TAKE TO HEART IS THAT TALENT ALONE IS NOT ENOUGH.

The most important takeaway I hope you take to heart is that talent alone is not enough. You cannot rely solely on your ability, no matter how good you are, or you'll never become the best artist you can be. **That's why I want to leave you with the mantra "Talent +", and I mean exactly that: It's not enough to just be talented. You need to be inspired and motivated to give more.**

This book has been a way to show you that, yes, of course, you need to have ability, an affinity for the art form, a love of taking class and learning. *However, you need much more – you need everything that goes into the "+" section.*

I hope you take the building blocks I've given you here

and use them to your advantage.

*Remember:*

**Class.** Show up on time and be prepared. Where you stand, how you relate to others, how you respond to the teachers — all of this matters. Work on presenting yourself well throughout your time there.

**Work ethic.** The most important question to ask yourself is, "**How much do you want to invest in yourself?**" Work ethic is where you're going to prove how great a dancer and artist you can be. The amount of work you put in equals the amount you're going to get from all your effort. This takes discipline and real determination, and it's all in your hands. You're in charge of how hard you're going to work in class every day. Be your own best boss!

**Reputation.** Work ethic and reputation go hand in hand. In a challenging career like ballet, or any kind of dance, people seek out the most dedicated workers to cast and choreograph on and have in the studio. Those artists are reliable, and the ones who will continue to improve, because they are constantly striving to be better. Your reputation follows you wherever you go in this career, so make sure that people remember you for all the right reasons.

**Good manners.** In spite of the perception that ballet dancers are divas, most are not, because diva-like behaviour is not welcome in class, in the rehearsal studio, or onstage. Come to think of it, that kind of behaviour in regular life isn't easy to take, either. Set an example by being kind and appreciative, because good manners can take you far.

**"Always a student."** Remember, you want to be moving forward, learning more, growing, and expanding not only your technique and artistry but also your experience. Who you are matters, because it gives your dancing shape, form, and maturity.

Keep in mind that **trying new styles**, getting **more**

**stage time**, **positivity**, and **confidence** can go a long way. Eating right, organizing your time, and the other tips I've given you will hopefully contribute to your growth, strength, and love for this incredible art form. I hope my advice has helped you think about how important it is for you to take charge of what you're doing. This takes a lot of courage and strength, but you will learn so much about yourself as each year passes.

Remember that **every mistake is not a failure** but rather a brief moment that presents you with an opportunity to learn. If you grow from your mistakes, they will propel you forward. They will only define you if you give up and let them.

Finally, embrace who you are. The dance world has room for many types of ballerinas. Don't waste your time worrying about what you don't have that others do; instead, focus that time and energy on making yourself the best dancer you can be. People want to hire a dedicated worker who can get along with others, someone striving to be better.

I truly believe that dancing is one of the most thrilling careers, and I would tell anyone who thinks they might want to dance to go for it! If you love it, there is no better feeling and form of expression. Whether you're shy or outgoing, the ability to express yourself through movement is a universal language everyone can understand. *There's nothing like it! Dance is the closest thing you can do to feel like you're flying!*

I want you to know you're not alone — I am here for you.

I am your Ballerina Big Sis! XO

*Love,*
*Tiler*

# TILER'S HACKS AND TIPS

# DANCE-BAG BASICS

## *Ballet Slippers*

**There are two basic categories here for ballet slippers: leather or canvas.** A lot of people now wear canvas and consider leather kind of "old school". But what I love about leather is that it really makes the dancer work all the muscles in the foot.

Unless it's mandatory to wear canvas shoes at your school, I would recommend leather because I think it will help strengthen and work your feet.

## *Pointe Shoes and Toe Pads*

**Pointe shoes are very specific to each dancer.** They are quite expensive, and every dancer will have a different preference. No matter what brand you decide to wear, make sure your pointe shoe looks like an extension of your foot. You do not want to pick a pointe shoe that looks bulky on your foot or doesn't allow you to roll through your metatarsals easily.

*What you wear in your pointe shoe is also completely individual.* Some people wear **no padding**, some wear just **lamb's wool** over their toes, and some wear **paper towels** over their toes to help absorb the sweat and allow the dancer to really feel the floor. Other people prefer an **Ouch Pouch**, a toe-pad cushion that offers protection in the area where dancers can develop bunions.

There are also **PerfectFit** toe pads made of a putty that moulds to your foot when you go on pointe.

The choice is up to you for how much padding you want to wear. Just know that there are many options for you to try.

HAVING A POINTE SHOE THAT IS MALLEABLE ALLOWS YOU TO DO DEMI-POINTE, WHICH IS CRITICAL TO HELPING YOU ROLL THROUGH YOUR FOOT BETTER.

## *Footcare Necessities*

There are certain things in my dance bag that are absolutely necessities, and 2nd Skin is one of them. I always carry 2nd Skin squares because they are great for blisters, actually life-changing!

They make several different products to prevent blisters and protect sensitive areas.

Some dancers even put surgical spirit into a little spritzer and spray it in places where the toe shoe still feels too hard. If your toe feels too firm, spraying a little bit of spirit around areas where the shoe needs to be able to bend is a great trick of the trade. Having a pointe shoe that is malleable allows you to do demi-pointe, which is critical to helping you roll through your foot better. **This will help strengthen your feet and your pointe work**. If you don't have surgical spirit handy, don't worry. Water works in the same way!

*If you're looking to prevent corns*, definitely keep some lamb's wool in your bag. You can put it in between your toes so they're not touching each other and causing irritation. People also use a makeup sponge in between their toes to prevent rubbing. Since the makeup sponge is wedge shaped, it fits perfectly and creates the space you need. You can also get a thin gel toe spacer, which is something I use. *As long as you put a little something in between the toes that are bothering you, less rubbing will help prevent corns.*

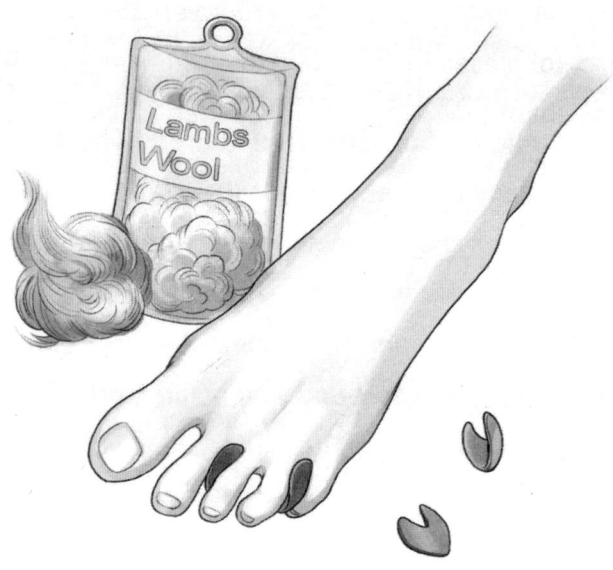

Bruised toenails can be extremely painful when you put on your pointe shoe and pressure is applied to that area. You can wear **Clear Stretch Tips**, made of clear gel, over your toes to help prevent this problem. I always wear them over my big toe, but you can wear them over any toes that need protection since they come in many different sizes.

Sometimes, if you have a really badly bruised toenail, you can use orthopaedic adhesive felt that is sticky on the bottom, with felt on top, to help. You make a little square by cutting four very thin horizontal pieces (two the length of the toenail, two the height of the toenail) that you then place in a square around the toenail to make a protector. **This can give your bruised nail some protection**, as there won't be any pressure now on it from the shoe.

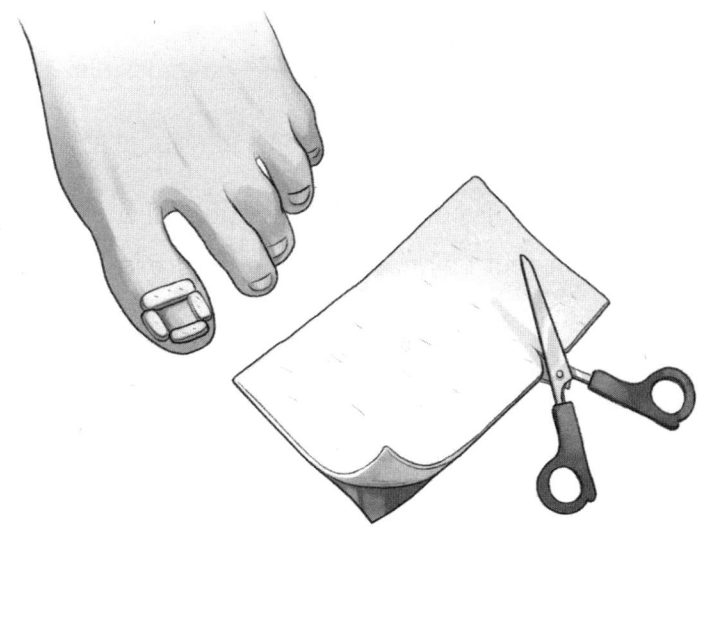

## *Toe-Shoe Sewing Kit and Accessories*

**One of my best little tricks for sewing shoes is using dental floss instead of thread.** Floss is very strong and doesn't break. So I always carry dental floss along with a little needle (that fits perfectly inside the floss box so you never lose it) and I am always prepared to sew. You'll need a pair of scissors as well as elastics and ribbons. There are many different kinds of elastics and ribbons that dancers use. Try to pick one that closely matches your tights so that the ribbons and elastics almost disappear. This way you can showcase your beautiful arch and foot in the best way possible.

I do have a certain way I like to tie my ribbons. I was taught to tie them with the inside ribbon going on top of the outer one when I cross them over my ankles. My teacher said this method would make the line look the most refined. So, I always make certain that the inside ribbon goes on the top when I tie my shoes.

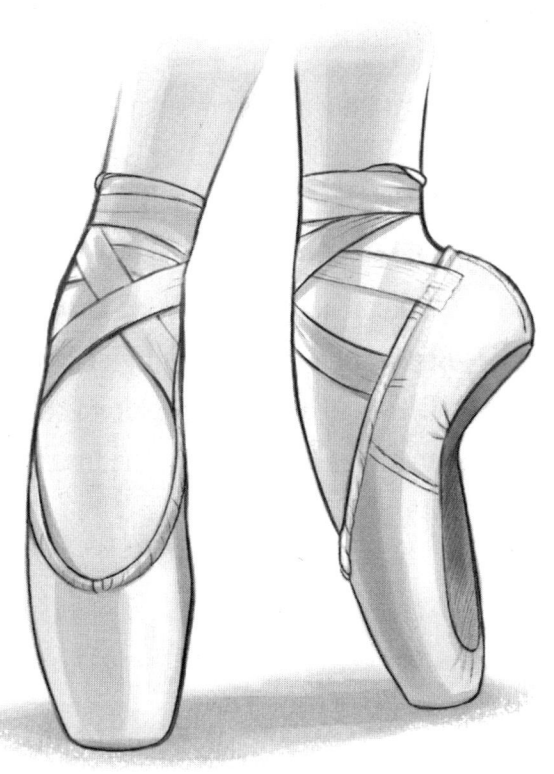

*Everybody uses elastic, of course, but there are many options available.* My favourite is **invisible mesh elastic** because I think it is less distracting to the eye. By blending in, it creates a cleaner look that allows your foot to show through. The attention needs to be on your foot, not on the elastic and ribbon.

## Massage Balls

First, you need a little rubber bouncy ball – you can find these in most corner shops, or buy a pack of them online for a pound or two. The ball needs to have a little squish and not be too hard. This makes it good for rolling out the bottoms of your feet when those muscles get very tight. You have to be very careful not to bruise your foot if you're rolling it too much on a hard ball. That's why a bouncy ball is great, because it has a little give.

Then, you need a bigger ball, like a tennis ball, which is great for rolling out your calves and glutes. Before class, I like to roll out my calves because it loosens up my muscles and allows my foot to point to its fullest.

Another useful tool to carry with you is a Pilates blow-up ball. This doesn't take up much room in your bag, because it is inflatable. You can make it as hard or soft as you need by filling it with the right amount of air. You can exercise different areas with it, such as abs, legs, or core; I like to place this ball in the middle of my upper spine and arch over it to help open up and stretch that area.

## *Therabands*

Therabands are **elastic resistance bands** that dancers use before class to warm up their feet. We use them to strengthen the toes by doing flex and point exercises against the resistance. You can also use a Theraband or a belt to lie on your back, lift your leg up in the air, and stretch your hamstrings.

## Hair Grips

**Hair grips are essential to keep your hair up.** I like to use long hair grips because they really help hold the hair. They're sold online and described as "bold, U-shaped" pins or grips. I am not sure many students use these, but it's what we use in the company, and they work very well!

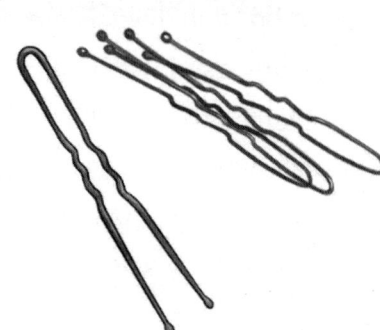

## Warm-ups

Sometimes, you need something handy to put on after class so you don't get cold after sweating. Tuck a **sweatshirt** and some **leggings** into your bag to pull on when you're finished. And of course, you need **leg warmers**, and warm-up booties to keep your legs and feet warm during breaks.

## Snacks

**Fuelling your body is essential when doing any high-performance activity.** It's smart to carry some snacks that you can easily eat on the go. Always have a protein bar and a fruit, such as an apple, pear, or banana in your bag. And always carry some long-lasting snacks, such as dried fruit and nuts. Even salty snacks are good if you try to choose healthier options, such as lentils or cauliflower chips. Try to prepare some small snacks you can toss in your bag that will help you stay fuelled and nourished while you are pushing your body.

## *Hydration*

**The most important thing you can do for your body when you're working hard in class is to make sure you're hydrated.** This is something I continue to work on myself as it's critical for our health and wellbeing to drink enough water. Our bodies are made up mainly of water, and working and sweating cause a real deficit. Dehydration can cause symptoms that would make it very difficult to dance. After all, you don't want to feel light-headed – that might lead to passing out. Keep a water bottle with you in your bag at all times and refill it often throughout the day. Drink about half a litre (that's two glasses of water) before breakfast and aim for at least half a glass every hour you're working in class.

> IT'S CRITICAL FOR OUR HEALTH AND WELLBEING TO DRINK ENOUGH WATER.

## *My Favourite Dance Bag*

Now that you know all my recommended necessities, you might wonder, where do I put them? My absolute favourite dance bag is the Só Dança Cali Backpack. The Cali Backpack is super roomy, so it holds everything and has lots of compartments to keep it all well-organized. The many different sections and zippered pockets make it easy for me to find what I need. There are even pouches for my water bottles on the outside and a sleeve inside for my iPad or laptop. Best of all, the Cali has straps that allow you to carry it as a tote bag on your arm or over your shoulders like a backpack, which is great for posture.

# TOE-SHOE TUTORIAL

*"How do I prep my pointe shoes?"*

Professional dancers have a much easier time with pointe shoes because they don't have to pay for them. It's a different story for students.

> SOME DANCERS WANT TO "FEEL THE FLOOR", AS WE SAY, SO THEY DON'T NEED THE TIP OF THE BOX TO BE HARDER, BUT THAT IS DEFINITELY A PERSONAL PREFERENCE.

I know that pointe shoes are **very expensive** and that families have a hard time paying to replenish them. So these tips should apply when a student is going to perform. Since the banging technique I use to quiet pointe shoes also makes them die faster, *make sure you use it wisely with that info in* *mind*. A family member might tell you, "These are really expensive. Please don't do anything to help them die quicker." So if you're not a professional dancer yet, make sure to remember that.

**One thing that helps pointe shoes last longer is Jet Glue.** This works by making the pointe shoe harder wherever you put the glue; however, *using glue also makes the shoes louder*.

I always put Jet Glue in the tip of my pointe shoes – the part that will touch the floor when on pointe. The glue goes there because I don't like to feel my toenails on the floor when on pointe. Some dancers want to "feel the floor", as we say, so they don't need the tip of the box to be harder. All dancers have their own personal preferences.

# WHEN YOU FEEL YOUR SHOES ARE GETTING SOFTER, YOU CAN APPLY GLUE TO SPECIFIC AREAS TO HELP GIVE THE SHOES A SECOND LIFE.

*You can use it as a sort of "lifesaver".*

When you feel your shoes are getting softer, you can apply glue to specific areas to help give the shoes a second life and last a bit longer. Often, I will Jet Glue my toe shoes the day after a performance so I can continue using them for some rehearsals. In particular, when using the glue, if you trace along the edges of the shank on the inside or outside of the shoe, it will help your shoes last longer. Most people glue the shank on the outside, but I like to glue it on the inside so I don't run the risk of the glue making the bottom of the shoe more slippery. I pour the glue on the inside of the shoe, along the edges of the shank, until just below my arch. If you feel your shoe isn't giving you support, gluing can help, and it's definitely worth a try. But remember, don't use too much! A little goes a long way. **And make sure to ask a more experienced dancer or a teacher to help when trying this for the first time.**

> THE SECRET TO QUIETING NEW POINTE SHOES IS BANGING THEM A LITTLE ON A WALL. IF THEY ARE STILL LOUD, GO BACK FOR ANOTHER ROUND.

*For a performance, I never just put on and wear a brand-new pair of pointe shoes.*

I have to work to make them quieter. You may have seen me on Instagram, banging my toe shoes on the concrete wall backstage. Wherever I go, I'm known for doing this, and now you can do it, too. I'm here to share my secret recipe for quiet shoes, so listen up!

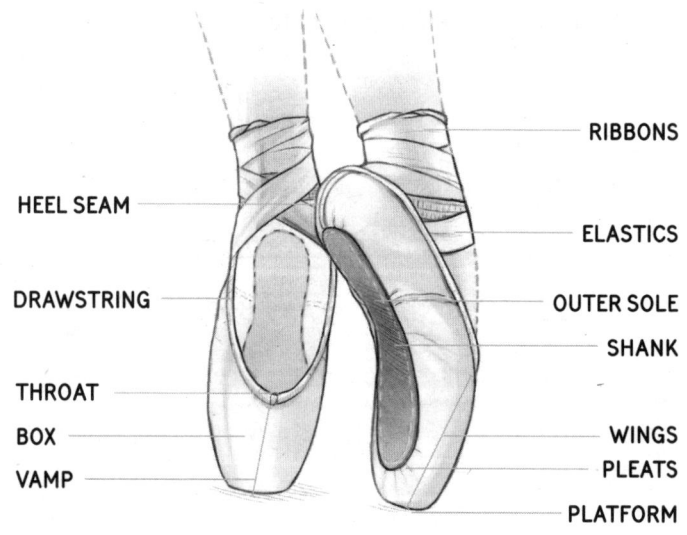

*Here's how it works.*

On the bottom of the shoe, there is the **shank**, and then there is the space right above it that leads to where the pointe shoe platform is. Try to think of the part of the shoe that hits the floor when you're running around on demi-pointe or landing from a jump. If you look at the pointe shoe diagram, it's the area where the pleats are shown on the bottom. That is the sweet spot that you want to bang on the wall to help the shoes be quiet during performance. Make sure that you are hitting the bottom of the shoe on the wall and not the top of the platform where you dance on pointe.

*I take the pointe shoe in my hand by holding on firmly to the shank to keep the shoe level, and then I start banging.*

You have to bang them quite hard, and how many times you do depends on the make of your shoe. Some types of pointe shoes may need a little, some may need a lot, and some might not need any at all. The secret to quieting new pointe shoes is banging them a little on a wall. If they are still loud, go back for another round.

> TO TEST IF MY POINTE SHOES ARE QUIET ENOUGH, I PUT THEM ON AND TAP MY FOOT ON THE FLOOR TO SEE IF I AM STILL MAKING NOISE.

Sometimes, you may notice that the banging will make the tip of the shoe look a little distorted; you might see the edge of the platform raised a little at the tip, where you need it to be flat to get on pointe. If this happens, do not fret! Just go back to the wall and do one or two light bangs right on the very tip of the shoe to make it level again.

*After I feel I have banged them enough, I walk to the stage and test them out.*

I put my pointe shoes on and tap my foot on the floor where I banged to see if I am still making noise. Sometimes the pointe shoes sound just right and I can put them away until the show; sometimes, they may still be a little too loud, and I have to go back for just a few more hits on the wall.

*I do this religiously, because I believe hearing a ballerina land from a jump or lift, or running around onstage, completely disrupts the ethereal atmosphere the dancers are trying to create.*

I think a ballerina should look as if everything she does is **effortless**. Her graceful beauty is what transports the audience, and any distraction can pull them out of the magic of the moment. So the last thing you want as a ballerina is for the audience to be more focused on your loud pointe shoes than on your dancing. And if you're an audience member, any disturbance can interrupt and distract from what you're watching. All of a sudden, you're thinking about how loud the pointe shoes sound instead of being transported by the incredible beauty of the performance.

> THE LAST THING YOU WANT AS A BALLERINA IS FOR THE AUDIENCE TO BE MORE FOCUSED ON YOUR LOUD POINTE SHOES THAN ON YOUR DANCING.

The same thing happens when I'm dancing – if I hear my own pointe shoes, all I can think about is how loud I am, and then I can't be fully present in what I'm dancing.

*So, here's what I would suggest if you're a student:*

Don't bang your shoes for class or variations, but when it comes time for a performance, you should try to quiet your shoes. Try testing the banging method for a rehearsal before a performance so you aren't doing it for the first time for a show. You will see what a difference it can make! In addition to helping with noise, banging your shoes also helps make them less slippery. Sometimes, in a newer pair of pointe shoes, you can catch an edge and might slip or fall. The banging isn't foolproof, but a rougher pleated bottom on the shoe is much safer than brand-new satin. Another tool some dancers use for a better grip is a pointe-shoe scraper, to roughen the sole. All of this will allow you to feel more grounded and confident in the shoes, which will then allow you to dance more freely.

I KNOW A LOT OF BALLERINAS PREP THEIR SHOES DIFFERENTLY, BUT I WOULD SAY THAT THESE TECHNIQUES HAVE BEEN REALLY HELPFUL AND I WISH SOMEONE HAD TOLD ME ABOUT THEM EARLIER.

*Another hack for your pointe shoes has to do with how much rosin you use.*

In my experience, you do not need a lot of rosin to get the best results. It matters more where and how you apply it. Unfortunately, I see a lot of students put rosin all over their pointe shoes, way too much. What we do at New York City Ballet, which is a great insider tip, is we use kitchen roll to cover our fingers, and then we rub it in the rosin and kind of "paint" the pointe shoe in areas where we think it would be most slippery.

You can start with the box, paint the top of it (just above the platform on the front of the shoe), and then turn it over and paint right along the sides of the shanks. And of course you need to paint on the part I said to bang, between the shank and the platform. *That's not a lot of rosin, but it's being used in all the right places.*

*Again, these are all my personal preferences.*

I know a lot of ballerinas do things differently, but these techniques have been really helpful and I wish someone had told me about them earlier.

## *Acknowledgements*

**Mom** – You are the reason I am who I am, and not just the dancer. You lead by example and show me that a woman can be both strong and loving at the same time. You have always expected 110 per cent from Myka and me, teaching us that if you work hard, dreams and goals become limitless. I am in awe of your strength and dedication to your family. You are my Wonder Woman!

**Dad** – You were always the biggest support system for your girls. I hope I am making you proud by trying to be a support system for the next generation of dancers as you were for me.

**Grandma** – You know you are the reason I am a ballerina. You drove me hours to make sure I received the best possible training, and without you, I would have never made it to where I am.

**Myka Chambers** – You might not have been my Ballerina Big Sis, but you were the best older sister, who taught me what it felt like to have someone to look up to and someone who would listen.

**Leslie Tonner Curtis** – You were the first person to come to me after seeing my Instagram series who said, "I think you have a book here." Thank you for always believing in me and bringing my words to life. Your love for the art form is truly profound, and your partnership on this book was an absolute gift!

**Lauren Auslander** – Thank you for always thinking big, far greater than I allow myself to do. You have truly stayed by my side as you continue taking me to new heights. You help me realize my dreams and then push me to dream beyond what I think is possible so you can make it happen.

**Lacy Lynch** – Thank you for always taking my ideas and knowing where to place them. I value your creativity and guidance more and more with every book. I know how much you believe in the power of storytelling, and I appreciate all you have done to make sure mine was heard.

**To my House of Story team, Dabney Rice, Alexandria Kominsky & Emily Easton** – I have always thought in order to succeed, you must surround yourself with inspiring people who are wiser than you, and know how to challenge you to achieve your best. You three are that, and I am so grateful that you were the team I had by my side throughout this process. Emily, I want to give a special shout-out to you for your dedication to this book. I will never forget the late hours we spent working on this together. Thank you for your time, expertise, and guidance.

**To my DK team in the US and across the pond, Katy Flint, Gayley Avery, Jennifer Brunn, Sara Forster, Hazel Eriksson & James Atkinson** – This book would not exist without you. You believed in my idea and brought it into being. You are the reason this book is reaching so many young dancers, and for that, I will never be able to thank you enough!

**Liz DeCesare & Alissa Goodman** – You are one dynamic duo. You came on board in the middle of this process and treated the book with such care. I feel very excited about my future with the two of you helping guide the way. Onwards!

**Tina James** – Thank you for coming up with the Ballerina Big Sis Instagram series. You showed me how many people connected to the topics we shared and sparked this idea for turning it into a book!

**Marika Molnar & Dr Thomas Novella** – To the best physical therapist and foot doctor, thank you for keeping all of us healthy and teaching us every trick of the trade to keep us on our toes.

**Roman Mejia** – Thank you for being the best dance partner not only onstage but also in life. You patiently listened to every thought, idea, and word I had for this book even before it was written on paper. You always gave me sound advice. I love you.

**Acquisitions Project Editor** Sara Forster
**Project Art Editor** Jon Hall
**Production Editor** Siu Yin Chan
**Senior Production Controller** Louise Minihane
**Senior Acquisitions Editor** Katy Flint
**Managing Art Editor** Vicky Short
**Art Director** Charlotte Coulais
**Managing Director** Mark Searle

Designed for DK by Anita Mangan
Text copyright © Tiler Peck, 2025
Artwork copyright © Sumiti Collina, 2025
Photo on page 6 by Erin Baiano

First published in Great Britain in 2025 by
Dorling Kindersley Limited
20 Vauxhall Bridge Road,
London SW1V 2SA

The authorised representative in the EEA is
Dorling Kindersley Verlag GmbH. Arnulfstr. 124,
80636 Munich, Germany

Copyright © 2025 Dorling Kindersley Limited
A Penguin Random House Company
10 9 8 7 6 5 4 3 2 1
002–349344–Oct/2025

All rights reserved. No part of this publication may be reproduced, stored in or introduced into a retrieval system, or transmitted, in any form, or by any means (electronic, mechanical, photocopying, recording, or otherwise), without the prior written permission of the copyright owner.
DK values and supports copyright. Thank you for respecting intellectual property laws by not reproducing, scanning or distributing any part of this publication by any means without permission. By purchasing an authorised edition, you are supporting writers and artists and enabling DK to continue to publish books that inform and inspire readers.
No part of this publication may be used or reproduced in
any manner for the purpose of training artificial intelligence technologies or systems. In accordance with Article 4(3) of the DSM Directive 2019/790, DK expressly reserves this work from the text and data mining exception.

A CIP catalogue record for this book
is available from the British Library.
ISBN 978-0-2417-3883-2

Printed and bound in the UK

**www.dk.com**

MIX
Paper | Supporting
responsible forestry
FSC™ C018179

This book was made with Forest Stewardship Council™ certified paper – one small step in DK's commitment to a sustainable future.
**Learn more at www.dk.com/uk/ information/sustainability**